THE TAFSĪR OF SŪRAH FĀTIHA

Commentary of Sūrah Fātiha

[The Opening Chapter of the Glorious Qur'ān]

SHAYKH ABDUL RAHEEM

Tafseer-Raheemi Publications 2017
First Edition: Sha'bān 1438/May 2017
ISBN: 978-1-912301-00-3

Author	Shaykh Abdul Raheem Limbādā (www.tafseer-raheemi.com)
Editing	Shaykh Abdul Raheem Limbādā
Transcribed by	Maulānā Ādam Sadak, Maulānā Junaid Bilāl, Maulānā Omer Anwar, Maulānā Abdullāh Patel, Maulānā Yūsuf Desai, Maulānā Arshad Bismillāh
Proofreading	Proofreading365 LLP (www.proofreading365.com), Ismail Amlā, Ahmed Bhūlā
Hadīth Referencing	Maulānā Omer Anwar
Cover Design	Muftī Abdur-Rahmān Mangera (www.zamzamacademy.com)
Typesetting	Belal Isakjee
Printed by	Mega Printers, Istanbul, Turkey (mega.com.tr)

Correspondence to the author or publishers may be sent to info@tafseer-raheemi.com

CONTENTS

1

3

FOREWORD

In the name of Allāh ﷻ, the Most Beneficent, the Most Merciful. Back in 2015, my most dearest and beloved teacher, Shaykh Abdul Raheem [Hāfizahullāh], expressed his desire to write the tafsīr of Sūrah Fātiha, after having written three previous publications; the tafsīr of Sūrah Yūsuf, which he completed in 2002; Sūrah Nūh, which was published in 2007; and most recently, the tafsīr of Sūrah Maryam which was made available in 2014.

A few years ago in Masjid-e-Qūbā, London, he delivered the tafsīr of Sūrah Fātiha in the Urdu language; which was carried out in the month of Ramadhān after the Asr prayer. An audio recording was taken and split into eight or nine parts.

The audio was sent to me to transcribe and to put this work into the form of a book. I realised what a huge responsibility this was going to be. Transcribing and translating this work from Urdu to the English language is no straightforward task. I asked Shaykh Abdul Raheem [Hāfizahullāh] if I could request some of my friends and colleagues to assist me in getting these translated, he gave me the go ahead. Alhamdulillāh, I received an excellent response from them, and they began working. The effort of their hard work is in front of you today.

Shaykh Abdul Raheem [Hāfizahullāh] then requested me to write some words as a form of gratitude and appreciation towards all those who helped with this work. At first, I felt my words were unworthy of inclusion, however, I really wanted to show my indebtedness towards all those that had helped put this work together.

I would like to sincerely thank all those who have assisted us with this work, especially Maulānā Ādam Sadak, Maulānā Junaid Bilāl, Maulānā Omer Anwar, Maulānā Abdullāh Patel, Maulānā Yūsuf Desai, and Maulānā Arshad Bismillāh who all played a part in transcribing. I would also like to thank the Proofreading365 team [Maulānā Nasrullāh Anwar, Maulānā Zakaryā Anwar and Maulānā Omer Anwar], not forgetting Brother Ismail Amlā, Ahmed Bhūlā, who assisted us in proofreading. Special thanks also to Muftī Abdur-Rahmān Mangera who gave some time out of his very busy schedule to go through the work with me and who provided some valuable guidance and feedback.

I pray that Allāh ﷻ forgives any errors that I have made whilst carrying out this work. I pray that Allāh ﷻ puts sincerity into all our hearts. I pray that Allāh ﷻ rewards these individuals in full, and takes this effort of theirs as a Sadaqah Jāriyah. May Allāh accept all the work that Shaykh Abdul Raheem [Hāfizahullāh] continues to do. May Allāh ﷻ give him the ability to write the tafāsir for the rest of the Qur'ān. May Allāh ﷻ be pleased with us all. Āmīn!

Belal Isakjee
21 Safar 1438
21 November 2016

PREFACE

بِسْمِ اللَّهِ الرَّحْمٰنِ الرَّحِيمِ

نحمده ونصلى على رسوله الكريم . اما بعد .

The Tafsīr you have before you was not written in a formal manner. Rather, it is a collection of discourses which I had delivered in Masjid-e-Qūbā in Stamford Hill, London, some years ago. Throughout the last ten days in the month of Ramadhān at the above Masjid, after the Asr prayer, I used to talk about the meaning and message of Sūrah Fātiha.

The speeches took place in Urdu. My dearest friend, [Maulānā] Belal Isakjee requested a group of his friends to assist him in translating these talks into English and preparing them for the wider audience. He divided different parts of these speeches between his friends.

Alhamdulillāh, they worked very quickly and the effort of their hard work is in yours hands.

I supplicate to Allāh ﷻ from the depth of my heart that Allāh ﷻ blesses each and every single one of them with His special Qurb. May Allāh ﷻ reward them for their efforts. May Allāh ﷻ fulfil their needs and be pleased with them. Āmīn!

I then edited the work which still needed many things adding. However, it was deemed better to publish what we have, rather than waiting to make more changes.

Since this was originally in the form of a speech, the mind of a speaker drifts from one subject to another. You will find many things which are not normally found in regular tafāsīr. Equally, you will find some things missing too. My thoughts were to go through a few tafāsīr and add a few things, which would have been very time consuming, so it was decided to publish what was available.

Detailed references cannot be given in speeches. My dearest friend, Maulānā Umar, son of our Sūfī Anwar Sāhib, went through the work whilst editing it and dug out the references. May Allāh ﷻ reward him for his hard work.

Let us hope and pray that this is a Fātiha [an opening] for the tafsīr of the rest of the Qur'ān and that Allāh ﷻ gives us the tawfeeq to write the tafsīr of the rest of the Qur'ān as well. Āmīn!

It is nothing hard for Allāh ﷻ. He takes work of deen from whoever He wills. Nothing is impossible for Him.

May Allāh ﷻ forgive our shortcomings. May Allāh ﷻ reward [Maulānā] Belal and his team. May Allāh ﷻ be pleased with us all. Āmīn!

[Shaykh] Abdul Raheem Limbādā [Hāfizahullāh]
22 Sha'bān 1437
30 May 2016

INTRODUCTION

Sūrah Fātiha is a makki sūrah. The sūrahs and verses of the Qur'ān that were revealed before the hijrah are called makki; the sūrahs and verses revealed after the Hijrah are called madani. Sūrah Fātiha was revealed in Makkāh Mukarramah.

Moreover, it is a sūrah which is recited many times a day in every salāh. Why is this? What message does Allāh ﷻ want to give to us in Sūrah Fātiha? It is a sūrah that Allāh ﷻ praises within the Qur'ān itself, stating in Sūrah Hijr:

$$وَلَقَدْ آتَيْنَاكَ سَبْعًا مِّنَ الْمَثَانِي وَالْقُرْآنَ الْعَظِيمَ ۞$$

We have given you the seven oft-repeated verses and the glorious Qur'ān. [1]

The phrase 'seven oft-repeated verses' indicates Sūrah Fātiha, as these are the seven verses that are recited most often. In this manner, Allāh ﷻ praises Sūrah Fātiha, announcing that *He* has revealed the 'seven oft-repeated verses', before mentioning the revelation of the rest of the 'Glorious Qur'ān' – asserting that Sūrah Fātiha is equal to the rest of the Qur'ān. This is indeed a magnificent sūrah.

It was also the very first sūrah to have been revealed in its entirety as a single revelation. It was most common that the Qur'ān would be revealed in parts, with a few select verses of a sūrah revealed at a time, such as with the lengthy Sūrah Baqarah. There are also some sūrahs, which were revealed in their entirety within one revelation, such as those short sūrahs that are found in the 30th Juz [Ammā Pārā]. However, Sūrah Fātiha was the very first sūrah to be revealed in its entirety. [2]

Prior to the revelation of Sūrah Fātiha, the first five verses of Sūrah 'Alaq and parts of the sūrahs Muzzammil and Muddathir respectively were sent

---

[1] Qur'ān 15:87.

[2] Seeratul Mustafā, Kāndhalwī.

down in revelation. Thereafter, Allāh ﷻ made the fulfilment of salāh an obligatory act and upon giving this command, revealed Sūrah Fātiha.

In fact, some Scholars state that Sūrah Fātiha is such a magnificent sūrah, that its revelation occurred twice. The first time it was brought down by Jibra'īl [Gabriel] ﷺ to the Prophet ﷺ whilst he was in Makkāh Mukarramah, and again, Jibra'īl ﷺ brought down this sūrah in revelation to the Prophet ﷺ after he migrated to Madīnah Munawwarah. [3]

In the tafsīr of Baidhāwī, it is mentioned that Sūrah Fātiha is known by fourteen different names. We understand that having many names is indicative of a high status and magnificence. In the way that Allāh ﷻ has 99 names, similarly, the Prophet ﷺ also has many names. As Jubair ibn Mut'im ﷺ narrates:

> Allāh's Messenger ﷺ said, "I have five names: I am Muhammad and Ahmad; I am Al-Māhī, through whom Allāh will eliminate infidelity; I am Al-Hāshir, who will be the first to be resurrected, the people being resurrected there after; and I am also Al-'Āqib [i.e. There will be no prophet after me]. [4]

In the same way, Sūrah Fātiha also has many names, one of which is Sūrah Fātihatil-Qur'ān, i.e. The Commencer of the Qur'ān. It is also known as Sūrah Ummul-Qur'ān, i.e. The Mother of the Qur'ān. The reason it is called the Mother of the Qur'ān is because Sūrah Fātiha is the summary of the entire Qur'ān. The entire Qur'ān and the meaning of it can be found summarized within just this one sūrah. The meaning of Sūrah Fātiha has then been expanded upon from Sūrah Baqarah onwards throughout the rest of the Qur'ān, making it 'Ummul Qur'ān [Mother of the Qur'ān]' as Sūrah Fātiha is the beginning point and the rest of the Qur'ān comes from/after it.

The Qur'ān consists of three matters; Beliefs, instructions, and the final ending of the good and of the bad. Sūrah Fātiha starts with Tawheed of Zaat

---

[3] Baidhāwī.
[4] Bukhārī: 3532, 4896; Muslim: 2354 b; Muwatta Mālik: 1861.

and Sifaat, i.e. that Allāh 🕮 is One and that He is attributed with all good attributes, which means He is free from all weaknesses. He is Allāh 🕮, the Rabb, the Rahmān, the Rahīm, and the Master of the Day of Judgement.

This Tawheed is the core of all beliefs. Once a person accepts the authority of Allāh 🕮, he will accept all other beliefs too. The reciter then accepts all instructions by declaring his devotion and seeking help in keeping up with that promise to worship Allāh 🕮 alone, and by seeking guidance and assistance, throughout this journey of devotion.

Then the final endings of the good and the bad, the fortunate and the wretched are mentioned. Stories of the previous prophets throughout the whole Qur'ān indicate towards this fact that the good had a better ending while the bad suffered the worst. The reciter begs Allāh 🕮 to let him learn by studying the Qur'ān and following the path of good, and avoiding that of the bad.

This sūrah is also called Sūrah Shifā, i.e. The sūrah of Healing. If this sūrah is prayed and blown upon a person suffering from an illness, Allāh 🕮 will cure him of his illness. Even the Prophet 🕮 has called this sūrah, Sūrah Shifā.

Once, a group of Sahābah 🕮 were travelling together and came upon a village where they stopped for a while. The people of that village were extremely miserly. The Sahābah 🕮 asked them if they would show some hospitality towards them and offer them any food and drink. But the villagers declined to show any hospitality whatsoever. The Sahābah 🕮 reminded them of their vow, which they had made to the Prophet 🕮 that should the army of the Prophet 🕮 come through the village, then they would show them hospitality and offer them food and drink, and the Sahābah 🕮 were indeed hungry and thirsty. Yet the villagers still refused and did not offer any welcome or generosity to the travelling Sahābah 🕮. The Sahābah 🕮 accepted their stance with patience and grace and prepared to travel onwards. It so happened that at that very moment, Allāh 🕮 had willed it so that the leader of their village was bit by a venomous snake. The villagers tried various different ways to treat and stop the toxic effect of the poison from spreading to the rest of his body, as if it were to reach the heart, it would result in death. They even made many attempts of reciting specific words and incantations, in accordance with their customs, and then blew on the affected limb with the hope that this would help, but to no avail. Their hearts were then inspired to approach the group of travelling Sahābah ﷺ, to ask if any among them had knowledge in *Ruqyah* with which they could help eliminate the poison. The Sahābah ﷺ responded saying, 'Yes, there are those among us that do have knowledge of this.' They were asked if they would help the village leader and, initially, the Sahābah ﷺ replied that they would not as they had not been hospitable or welcoming to them. However, after some insistence from the villagers, the Sahābah ﷺ agreed. In return the Sahābah ﷺ asked for a payment of thirty [30] goats. The villagers agreed.

Hadhrat Abu Saʿīd Al-Khudrī ﷺ [the narrator of the Hadīth] arrived and began to pray Sūrah Fātiha and upon completion, blew on the leader. He did this once, twice, thrice, each time praying and then blowing. He did this seven times and at the completion of the seventh attempt, the leader jumped up full of energy as though he was a prisoner that had just been released from his shackles. The damaging effect of the poison had vanished. The leader fulfilled the promise and handed over thirty goats to the Sahābah ﷺ.

The Sahābah ﷺ accepted the payment, however they began to wonder if what they had done by asking for a payment had been the right thing to do. The Sahābah ﷺ had done this because they knew that Islam would not disallow it, however, for their own peace of mind they wanted to ask the Prophet ﷺ. Upon reaching Madīnāh Munawwarah, they approached the Prophet ﷺ and related the entire story to him. The Prophet ﷺ responded by telling them that what they had done was correct and in fact, this is the way such miserly people should be dealt with. The Prophet ﷺ assured them that they did nothing wrong in taking the goats and asked them to share out the goats amongst themselves and that a share of the goats should come to him also. Hadhrat Abu Sa'īd Al-Khudrī ﷺ was then asked by the Prophet ﷺ about how he had come to know that Sūrah Fātiha was a means of curing the sick. The Prophet ﷺ then re-iterated that indeed Allāh ﷻ has placed in this sūrah a means of cure. [5]

Should you visit a person who is ill, pray Durūd Sharīf thrice, then Sūrah Fātiha seven times and then again Durūd Sharīf thrice and blow on them. Inshā-Allāh, they will be cured.

This sūrah is also called Sūrah Shāfiah, Sūrah Kāfiyah, Sūrah Wāfiah and like this, altogether fourteen names [14] are mention in Tafsīr Baidhāwī.

We now begin with the Tafsīr of this sūrah.

VERSE 1

$$ \text{﴿١﴾ الْحَمْدُ لِلَّهِ رَبِّ الْعَالَمِينَ} $$

All Praise belongs to Allāh, the Rabb of all the worlds.

Only Allāh ﷻ is worthy of being praised. The reason for this is because Allāh ﷻ is the Rabb of all the worlds. He is Al-Rahmān; the extremely Compassionate. He is Al-Rahīm; the extremely Merciful. He is the creator of everything and not only has He created all things but after creating it, He is the one ensuring that it continues to run perfectly. He controls and supervises all affairs and Allāh is in charge of all things.

Along with being Al-Rahman and Al-Rahīm, He is also the Rabb of the Day of Judgement. Allāh ﷻ is the One with all the power and authority. When the Day of recompense arrives, the Day of Judgement, every person who has ever lived will be made to rise and everyone will stand together. No person will be able to do as they please, no matter how much authority, power, or influence they had in this world. The likes of Fir'aun [Pharaoh], Hāmān, Namrūd

---

[5] Bukhārī: 2276, 5736, 5737.

[Nimrod], and Qārūn [Korah] will have no authority over anyone. "Every man for himself." Allāh ﷻ mentions in the Qur'ān regarding this in various places:

$$وَكُلُّهُمْ آتِيهِ يَوْمَ الْقِيَامَةِ فَرْدًا ۝$$

Each one of them will come to Him all alone on the Day of standing. [6]

Allāh ﷻ also mentions:

$$لِّمَنِ الْمُلْكُ الْيَوْمَ ۖ لِلَّهِ الْوَاحِدِ الْقَهَّارِ ۝$$

To Whom does the Kingdom belong today? To Allāh, the One, the Omnipotent. [7]

And:

$$يَوْمَ لَا تَمْلِكُ نَفْسٌ لِّنَفْسٍ شَيْئًا ۖ وَالْأَمْرُ يَوْمَئِذٍ لِّلَّهِ ۝$$

It shall be a day when no soul will be able to benefit another soul
in the least. On that day all authority will belong to Allāh. [8]

It will become clear to all those standing on the Day of Judgement that full control is with Allāh ﷻ. It is for these reasons that Allāh ﷻ alone is worthy of all praise.

The first word of this sūrah is '*Alhamdulillāh*', meaning that all praise [ta'reef] is due, only to Allāh ﷻ. To do 'ta'reef' is to praise someone on some achievement, attribute or deed. To do ta'reef is a means of showing gratitude and thanks. It is mentioned in a Hadīth that:

$$الْحَمْدُ رَأْسُ الشُّكْرِ ، مَا شَكَرَ اللَّهَ عَبْدٌ لَا يَحْمَدُهُ$$

"To praise is the root of showing gratitude. That person who

---

[6] Qur'ān 19:95.
[7] Qur'ān 40:16.
[8] Qur'ān 82:19.

does not praise Allāh, has not shown gratitude to Allāh." [9]

As an example, if someone were to present you with a gift, there are three ways in which you are to show gratitude for the gift you have received:

1. With the heart – This can be done through having sincere appreciation of the gift in the heart, and realising that the person thought about you and offered you the gift.

2. With the tongue – This can be done by saying words such as *'Jazākallāh'* and 'thank-you.' Be thankful with the tongue [saying thanks and offering Duās].

3. Through actions – By giving a gift in return to that person.

To accept a gift and then to return a gift with something even better than what was received was a habit of the Prophet ﷺ. It is also mentioned in a Hadīth that if you are able to give a gift in return then do so, if you are unable to do so, then say *'Jazākallāh'*. Saying *'Jazākallāh'* is also a way of returning a good favour. [10]

We should also show gratitude [Shukr] to Allāh ﷻ. This show of gratitude should be done with the heart, by appreciating each and every favour and blessing that has been blessed upon us by Allāh ﷻ. We should understand that everything we have, has been bestowed upon us by Allāh ﷻ. If we started counting the blessings of Allāh ﷻ, we would be unable to do so. We would become tired from counting, yet the bounties and blessings of Allāh ﷻ would not be covered because they are endless and innumerable. If we were to ponder for a while, we would come to realise just how many blessings Allāh ﷻ has bestowed upon us. First, we have the outer blessings that can be seen such as health, wealth, cars, job, money, etc. Then we have the *'Rūhāni"* [spiritual] blessings such as Īmān, Islam, Ihsān, Qur'ān, Prayer, Fasting, Zakāt, Hajj,

---

[9] Jāmi' Ma'mar bin Rāshid: 166; Baihaqī: (Shu'abul Īmān) 4079, (al-Ādāb) 708; Baghawī: (Sharhus Sunnah) 1256, (Tafsīr) 757.

[10] Bulūgh al-Marām: 1383; Ibn Hibbān: 3404; Tirmīdhī: 2035.

Hidāyah, these are all great blessings. Even breathing smoothly is a blessing from Allāh ﷻ and without it we would faint and eventually die. It is imperative to instil within ourselves a state which constantly remembers the blessings of Allāh ﷻ upon us. Allāh ﷻ asks us thirty-one [31] times in Sūrah Rahmān:

$$فَبِأَيِّ آلَاءِ رَبِّكُمَا تُكَذِّبَانِ ۞$$

"So which favours of your Lord [Rabb] will you then deny?" [11]

We should all take some time out during the day to sit in quiet contemplation in which we bow our heads and remember Allāh ﷻ and thank Him from the bottom of our hearts, and in this way we will come to a stage in which even in perceived hardships, we will find the blessings of Allāh ﷻ. When a person suffers from an illness, his sins are forgiven during this time of hardship and his rank is raised in the hereafter. So such a person will be grateful to Allāh ﷻ even in illness.

Both good health and illness are blessings from Allāh ﷻ. However, we have been taught by the Prophet ﷺ that we should ask for the blessing of good health and not the blessing of illness in our Duās as is mentioned in the Qur'ān:

$$رَبَّنَا آتِنَا فِي الدُّنْيَا حَسَنَةً وَفِي الْآخِرَةِ حَسَنَةً وَقِنَا عَذَابَ النَّارِ ۞$$

O our Rabb, grant us good in this world, good in the Akhirah,
and save us from the punishment of the fire. [12]

Do not ask for illness from Allāh ﷻ but should you ever be overcome by an illness, observe patience and ask Allāh ﷻ to restore your good health.

---

[11] Qur'ān 55: Multiple verses.
[12] Qur'ān 2:201.

Once, the Prophet ﷺ had just finished taking a bath and had put on some fresh clothing and applied some perfume. When he came to the gathering of the Sahābah, they commented on how well the Prophet ﷺ looked. The Prophet ﷺ praised Allāh ﷻ. The Sahābah ؓ were talking amongst themselves and specifically conversing with regards to the blessing of having money and how it was a good thing to have, and that it should not be wasted on frivolous things. At this point the Prophet ﷺ joined the conversation and said, 'There is no harm in wealth for someone who has piety [taqwā], but good health for one who has piety is better than riches, and being of good cheer is a blessing.' [13]

The reason for this is because a person with Taqwā [God-consciousness] will use the money wisely but a person without Taqwā would be inclined towards sin through this wealth and would spend the money in ways that will incur sin upon that person. The Prophet ﷺ further mentions, 'Good health for one who has piety is better than riches.' Thereafter the Prophet ﷺ said that a person who remains cheerful and happy has received an immeasurable blessing from Allāh ﷻ. The reason for this is because he will remain happy, cheerful and in a good mood in every state and will be content and happy with whatever Allāh ﷻ has blessed him with.

The ال in أَلْحَمْدُ لِلّٰهِ is for Istighrāq – it covers all praises. All praises we hear are directly or indirectly related to Allāh ﷻ. For example the sun is very bright, the moon looks beautiful and the stars are shining. In reality, all this praise returns to Allāh ﷻ because the sun and moon are all created and beautified by Allāh ﷻ.

Ability and power is all from Allāh ﷻ. If someone praises a Mercedes or a Rolls Royce, he is praising the manufacturer. The manufacturer was given the ability and the intellect by Allāh ﷻ, so the final praise returns back to Him. One Hadīth says:

---

[13] Ibn Mājah: 2224; Al-Adab Al-Mufrad: 301.

اَللّٰهُمَّ لَكَ الْحَمْدُ كُلُّهُ وَلَكَ الْمُلْكُ كُلُّهُ وَاِلَيْكَ يُرْجَعُ الْاَمْرُ كُلُّهُ

O Allāh, praise is for you, all of it. And Kingdom belongs to you, all of it.
And Khair is in your hand, all of it. And Matters return to you, all of them. [14]

Allāh ﷻ likes being praised. Nobody likes praise more than Allāh ﷻ. Generally, if someone is praised for doing something good and shown gratitude, they like it. In one Hadīth, Rasūlullāh ﷺ has said:

'There is none who likes praise more than Allāh. And because of that, Allāh has promised Jannah.' [15] [People should praise Him, and by doing this, they should try to attain Jannah].

In another Hadīth, it is said:

'The best form of Dhikr is 'Lā Ilāha Illal-llāh'
and the best form of Duā is 'Alhamdulillāh.' [16]

When you say Alhamdulillāh, in effect you are asking Allāh ﷻ for His bounty and grace because when you praise someone of a high status and they are of understanding, they know that this person is praising me because he is in need of something. Allāh ﷻ understands that His servants need something from Him and Allāh ﷻ fulfils our needs. Thus, saying Alhamdulillāh is also a form of asking and begging from Allāh ﷻ.

One Hadīth says:

وَالْحَمْدُ لِلَّهِ تَمْلَأُ الْمِيزَانَ . وَسُبْحَانَ اللَّهِ وَالْحَمْدُ لِلَّهِ تَمْلَآنِ
– أَوْ تَمْلَأُ – مَا بَيْنَ السَّمَوَاتِ وَالأَرْضِ

---

[14] Musannaf Abdur Razzāq: 5000; Marwazī: (Salātul-watr) 82; Ibn Abi-Dunyā: (Hawātiful-Jinān) 59; Tabrānī: (ad-Duā) 1641.

[15] Bukhārī: 7416; Muslim: 1499 a.

[16] Tirmīdhī: 3383; Ibn Mājah: 3800.

Alhamdulillāh fills the scale and 'Subhānallāh Walhamdulillāh'
[together] fill the space between the heavens and the earth. [17]

The scale could mean, the one which will be placed in the Maidān-e-Hashr for weighing the deeds of human beings. That huge scale can be filled with one sincere '*Alhamdulillāh*'.

In one Hadīth, one Sahābī ﷺ said the words:

يَا رَبِّ لَكَ الْحَمْدُ كَمَا يَنْبَغِي لِجَلَالِ وَجْهِكَ وَلِعَظِيمِ سُلْطَانِكَ

The Angels were uncertain and did not know how to write this down [as Allāh ﷺ was giving so much reward] so they ascended to heaven and said, 'O Allāh, your servant has praised you from the depths of his heart so much so that we are unable to write down the reward.' Allāh ﷺ asked regarding what he had said and they repeated the words. Allāh ﷺ said if you cannot record the reward, write down the words and I will reward him Myself on the day of Qiyāmah. [18]

As mentioned previously, Hamd [praise] is the root of shukr [thanksgiving] and a person who does not praise Allāh ﷺ has not done the shukr of Allāh ﷺ. Thus, if we want to be thankful, we need to praise Allāh ﷺ.[19] If we praise Allāh ﷺ and do shukr, Allāh ﷺ will give us more – this is the promise of Allāh ﷺ. Allāh ﷺ promises:

لَئِن شَكَرْتُمْ لَأَزِيدَنَّكُمْ ۞

"If you are grateful, I will give you more." [20]

---

[17] Muslim: 223; Tirmīdhī: 3517; Riyādh As-Sālihīn: 1413.

[18] Ibn Mājah: 3801; Ibn Kathīr.

[19] Jāmi' Ma'mar bin Rāshid: 166; Baihaqī: (Shu'abul Īmān) 4079, (al-Ādāb) 708; Baghawī: (Sharhus Sunnah) 1256, (Tafsīr) 757.

[20] Qur'ān 14:7.

THE MEANING OF RABB

The word رَب is from rubūbiyyah - meaning to nurture someone, or to bring someone up. Allāh ﷻ is Our Murabbi, He is Our Khāliq [Creator]. He protects us and takes care of us. Allāh ﷻ Is Our Rabb. True praise is for Allāh ﷻ who creates, who nurtures, and who protects. The word Rabb is also derived from tarbiyyah. Tarbiyyah means 'to look after', 'to bring up', and 'the one who controls'. So Rabb is a seegha [Arabic case or formula] of sifat mushabbah [adjectival or attributive participle] on the scale of sa'bun [صعب].

Allāh ﷻ is the one who created the dunya and He is the one who is keeping everything in control on a daily basis. The Qur'ān mentions:

$$\text{يَسْأَلُهُ مَن فِي السَّمَاوَاتِ وَالْأَرْضِ ۚ كُلَّ يَوْمٍ هُوَ فِي شَأْنٍ ۞}$$

*"All in the heavens and the earth ask from Him
and He is engaged in some matter every day."* [21]

RABB IS ALWAYS BUSY

Allāh ﷻ is always busy in His work, He is not such to create and then abandon His creation. He is always busy looking after them. The Prophet ﷺ has said: 'Indeed, Allāh ﷻ does not sleep, nor is it befitting for Him to sleep. The actions of the day reach Him before the [commencement of] the actions of the night and the actions of the night reach Him before [the commencement of] the actions of the day. The veil of Allāh ﷻ is of nūr [light]. If Allāh ﷻ was to remove the veil, the rays of His Essence/Being would burn and destroy every creation as far as His sight would reach.' [22] [And there is nothing out of His sight].

---

[21] Qur'ān 55:29.

[22] Muslim: 179 a; Ibn Mājah: 200, 201.

So Allāh ﷻ is the All Mighty God. He is our Rabb; He looks after the whole world. He is Al Hayy [Ever Living] and He is Al Qayyūm [The One Who Sustains]. Since He does all these things, He is attributed with the sifat of Rabb.

PHARAOH'S CLAIM OF RABB

Pharaoh used to propagate that he himself was the Rabb. He used to say that it was fine that people were worshipping the smaller idols, but he used to tell them to remember that he was the greatest Rabb and that he was the only one that was worthy of being worshipped. He would claim:

$$أَنَا رَبُّكُمُ الْأَعْلَىٰ ۞$$

I am your highest Rabb. [23]

From the outset, Mūsā ﷺ attacked this claim of his, by saying:

$$رَبُّ السَّمَاوَاتِ وَالْأَرْضِ وَمَا بَيْنَهُمَا ۞$$

'My Rabb is the Rabb of the heavens and the earth and whatever is in between.' [24]

Mūsā ﷺ said to Pharaoh that I am calling you towards that Being. Pharaoh turned to his people and said:

$$أَلَا تَسْتَمِعُونَ ۞$$

"Do you hear what he says?" [25]

Mūsā ﷺ then says:

$$رَبُّكُمْ وَرَبُّ آبَائِكُمُ الْأَوَّلِينَ ۞$$

---

[23] Qur'ān 79:24.

[24] Qur'ān 26:24.

[25] Qur'ān 26:25.

He [Allāh] is Your Rabb and the Rabb of your ancestors. [26]

Pharaoh then says:

$$إِنَّ رَسُولَكُمُ الَّذِي أُرْسِلَ إِلَيْكُمْ لَمَجْنُونٌ ۞$$

Indeed your Rasūl [Messenger] who has been sent to you is certainly insane. [27]

Mūsā ﷺ replied by saying:

$$رَبُّ الْمَشْرِقِ وَالْمَغْرِبِ وَمَا بَيْنَهُمَا ۞$$

He is the Rabb of East and West and whatever is in between them. [28]

Pharaoh did not want to hear this so he replied by saying:

$$لَئِنِ اتَّخَذْتَ إِلَٰهًا غَيْرِي لَأَجْعَلَنَّكَ مِنَ الْمَسْجُونِينَ ۞$$

If you take another as an Ilaah besides myself, I shall definitely make you among the prisoners. [29]

Instead of trying to understand, Pharaoh threatens him with jail. Mūsā ﷺ says:

$$أَوَلَوْ جِئْتُكَ بِشَيْءٍ مُّبِينٍ ۞$$

Even if I bring you some sign very clear? [30]

Pharaoh replies by saying:

$$فَأْتِ بِهِ إِن كُنتَ مِنَ الصَّادِقِينَ ۞$$

---

[26] Qur'ān 26:26.

[27] Qur'ān 26:27.

[28] Qur'ān 26:28.

[29] Qur'ān 26:29.

[30] Qur'ān 26:30.

Bring it if you are truthful. [31]

Pharaoh told Mūsā ﷺ to bring some signs if he was from amongst the truthful ones. This was the first meeting between them. The Qur'ān states:

$$\text{فَأَلْقَىٰ عَصَاهُ فَإِذَا هِيَ ثُعْبَانٌ مُّبِينٌ ❁}$$

So he threw down his staff and it suddenly became a manifest serpent. [32]

Mūsā ﷺ dropped his staff and it became a great serpent. It opened its mouth and started slithering towards Pharaoh. Pharaoh jumped off his throne and hid behind it screaming for help.

Everyone has a little fear of snakes, who doesn't? Mūsā ﷺ at first also got scared of this snake. The Qur'ān states:

$$\text{قَالَ خُذْهَا وَلَا تَخَفْ ۖ سَنُعِيدُهَا سِيرَتَهَا الْأُولَىٰ ❁}$$

Allāh said, 'Grab hold of it and do not be afraid.
We shall soon return it to its original state.' [33]

Allāh ﷻ had to reassure Mūsā ﷺ.

Pharaoh was also frightened and alarmed. There was chaos in his court, everyone was running around. Mūsā ﷺ grabbed the snake and it returned to its original state. Mūsā ﷺ said look at the other sign:

$$\text{وَنَزَعَ يَدَهُ فَإِذَا هِيَ بَيْضَاءُ لِلنَّاظِرِينَ ❁}$$

And he withdrew his hand, which instantly turned white for all to see. [34]

---

[31] Qur'ān 26:31.

[32] Qur'ān 26:32.

[33] Qur'ān 20:21.

[34] Qur'ān 26:33.

Mūsā﷿ then put it back in and it returned to its original state. These were the miracles of the prophets. Pharaoh then called for the magicians. He said that this man is a magician, so we will fight magic with magic.

In this story we heard the description of Rabb in the words of one of His greatest prophets. This is my Rabb, who does all these things, the Rabb of the heavens and the Rabb of the earth. The Rabb of the East and Rabb of the West and whatever is between them, He is the true Controller and the One Who takes care of all affairs.

DUᾹ'S OF THE PROPHETS WHICH INCLUDE THE SIFAT OF 'RABB'

When various prophets would make Duā, they would call upon Allāh ﷻ with the sifat 'Rabb'. Adam﷿ says:

$$رَبَّنَا ظَلَمْنَا أَنْفُسَنَا وَإِن لَّمْ تَغْفِرْ لَنَا وَتَرْحَمْنَا لَنَكُونَنَّ مِنَ الْخَاسِرِينَ ۞$$

'O our Rabb! We have harmed ourselves and if You do not forgive us and show mercy to us, we will surely be of the losers.' [35]

Nūh ﷿ said:

$$رَبِّ إِنِّي أَعُوذُ بِكَ أَنْ أَسْأَلَكَ مَا لَيْسَ لِي بِهِ عِلْمٌ$$

$$وَإِلَّا تَغْفِرْ لِي وَتَرْحَمْنِي أَكُن مِّنَ الْخَاسِرِينَ ۞$$

'O my Rabb! I seek Your protection from asking You for things regarding which I have no knowledge. If you do not forgive me and have mercy on me, I will be of the losers.' [36]

Ibrāhim﷿ said:

$$رَبِّ اجْعَلْنِي مُقِيمَ الصَّلَاةِ وَمِن ذُرِّيَّتِي ۞$$

'O my Rabb! Make me one who establishes salāh, as

---

[35] Qur'ān 7:23.
[36] Qur'ān 11:47.

well as from my progeny [those who establish salāh].' [37]

Mūsā ﷺ said:

رَبِّ إِنِّي ظَلَمْتُ نَفْسِي فَاغْفِرْ لِي ۞

'O my Rabb! I have wronged myself, so forgive me.' [38]

There are many other examples in the Qur'ān from many prophets. They called upon Him with the sifat of 'Rabb' when supplicating.

WE SHOULD ALSO CALL UPON HIM WITH 'RABBANĀ'

Allāh ﷻ also encourages us to call upon him with the sifat Rabb. He teaches us the Duā's in the Qur'ān:

رَبَّنَا لَا تُؤَاخِذْنَا إِن نَّسِينَا أَوْ أَخْطَأْنَا ۞

O our Rabb, do not take us to task if we forget or make mistakes. [39]

And:

رَبَّنَا هَبْ لَنَا مِنْ أَزْوَاجِنَا وَذُرِّيَّاتِنَا قُرَّةَ أَعْيُنٍ وَاجْعَلْنَا لِلْمُتَّقِينَ إِمَامًا ۞

'O our Rabb! Grant us the coolness of our eyes from our spouses and children and make us Imaams of the pious.' [40]

And:

رَبَّنَا لَا تُزِغْ قُلُوبَنَا بَعْدَ إِذْ هَدَيْتَنَا وَهَبْ لَنَا

مِنْ لَدُنْكَ رَحْمَةً ۚ إِنَّكَ أَنْتَ الْوَهَّابُ ۞

---

[37] Qur'ān 14:40.

[38] Qur'ān 28:16.

[39] Qur'ān 2:286.

[40] Qur'ān 25:74.

*'Our Rabb, do not cause our hearts to stray after You have
guided us. Grant us Your mercy for verily You are the Great Giver.'* [41]

So these Duās have been taught to us with the wording 'Rabbanā' [Our Rabb],
because Allāh ﷻ dearly loves to be called upon with the call of Rabbanā. This
is why He has mentioned the sifat/quality/attribute of Rabb here. The
Sustainer, the Controller and the Guardian of all the worlds is Allāh ﷻ. This is
how we should praise Allāh ﷻ and then we should proceed to ask of our needs.

OUR RABB CARES FOR THE WHOLE WORLD

Allāh ﷻ looks after you and me. He looks after everyone. To understand this,
let me give you an example. Once, I boarded a plane and as soon as we took off,
we could see all the houses beneath us. I started to think of the many people
who would be living in all those houses. There would be men, women and
children, young and old, healthy and ill – all living there. If the responsibility
of looking after all these people was given to one person, they would never be
able to carry it out. He would have to provide for them, look after their needs,
nurture them, sustain them, put them to sleep and awaken them. Only Allāh
ﷻ is capable of doing all this.

Allāh ﷻ is watching us right now. He knows each person that is reading this
book at this very moment in time. He knows what each of us is thinking, and
what is happening in the lives of each and every one of us. One of us may be
suffering from aching limbs. One may have arthritis; another may have
heartache, headache, or a bad stomach. Allāh ﷻ knows every minute detail.
Allāh ﷻ created the whole universe and created it correctly without any faults.

---

[41] Qur'ān 3:8.

OUR RABB'S WISDOM IN CREATION

Once, an agnostic walked through a garden. In this garden were wonderful watermelons. He sat under a cherry tree that had small cherries growing on it. He started thinking to himself that how can there be a god when things are misplaced in the world? Here we have such a small fruit growing on a giant tree, and over there, there are massive watermelons growing on such a small bush. The correct way would be to put the big watermelons upon the big trees, and these tiny cherries upon those small bushes.

As he was thinking this, a cherry fell off the tree and hit him on the head! He thought to himself what has happened here? When pondering further, he thought that there must be a god! If in the place of a cherry, a watermelon was to hit me on the head, it could have killed me. It is correct how it is. The cherry being on the tree is as perfect as the watermelon being on the ground.

THE MEANING OF ĀLAMĪN

Allāh ﷻ created the whole world and He is the one looking after it all. This is why we say:

$$\text{الْحَمْدُ لِلَّهِ رَبِّ الْعَالَمِينَ ۞}$$

'Ālamīn is the plural of 'Ālam. 'Ālam is a known world. There is an 'Ālam of humanity, 'Ālam of animals, and also of Jinns, Angels and fishes etc. Each and every species is known as an 'Ālam. However many 'Ālams Allāh ﷻ has created, Allāh ﷻ is the One Who is the Rabb of them all. He is the Controller and one who looks after them. He is in charge of the Angels, the Jinn, the birds and looking after the fish in the sea. It is all in His Hands.

Ibn Kathīr ﷽ writes that 'Ālamīn includes everything, besides Allāh ﷻ, that exists in the universe. It is the plural of 'Ālam and 'Ālam is a plural that has no singular from its wording. Awālim are all the creations in the heavens, on the land, and in the oceans. Zujāj ﷽ says, 'Ālam means everything Allāh ﷻ has created in the dunya and in the ākhirah [Hereafter].' Qurtubī ﷽ says

29

that this is the more appropriate tafsīr because ʿĀlam is from ʿAlāmat, meaning sign. The whole world is a sign of Allāh's ﷻ existence.

As a poet says:

فيا عجبا كيف يعصى الاله . ام كيف يجحده الجاحد .

وفى كل شىء له اية . تدل على انه واحد .

'Amazing! How can God be disobeyed? And how can a denier deny Him when
in every creation there is a sign which indicates that He is the only one?'

A STORY OF SULAIMĀN ﷺ

Sulaimān ﷺ was a great messenger of Allāh ﷻ. Allāh ﷻ gave him the ability to talk to the animals, jinn and angels. Allāh ﷻ granted him many blessings and wealth, Sulaimān ﷺ was very thankful.

Once Sulaimān ﷺ asked Allāh ﷻ if he could prepare a feast for all the creatures. He was granted permission by Allāh ﷻ. Sulaimān ﷺ prepared a giant meal and the dastarkhwān [banquet] spread for miles and miles. He called out to all the creatures to come and partake of this tremendous meal. As he called out, a giant whale-like fish leapt out of the sea and devoured everything that had been prepared in one bite! Sulaimān ﷺ was left amazed and asked Allāh ﷻ what had happened. The reply was that, 'O Sulaimān! I provide three times as much as what you made, for this fish alone on a daily basis.' [42]

Subhānallāh! That was just one meal of the day for that fish. It still needed two more of the same portions for that particular day.

We realise it is Allāh ﷻ and only Allāh ﷻ who feeds and looks after all the creation. Even if there was to be a tiny black insect in the middle of a rock, Allāh ﷻ will provide its sustenance.

---

[42] Makhzāne Akhlaaq.

A STORY OF MŪSĀ ﷺ

Once Mūsā ﷺ asked Allāh ﷻ to make his sustenance easy for him, so that he doesn't have to work too hard for it. Allāh asked, 'O Mūsā! Why are you worried about your sustenance?' He asked again 'Ya Allāh! So it becomes easier for me.' Allāh ﷻ said that let me show you a sign. Allāh ﷻ ordered him to strike a rock with his staff. Mūsā ﷺ struck it and it broke into two pieces, and another rock appeared from within it. He was ordered to strike it again. He did so and the same thing happened; it broke into two and another stone appeared from within it. He was then ordered to strike it for a third time. As he struck it, it crumbled and from within it, an insect came out which started to move. Allāh ﷻ ordered Mūsā ﷺ to bring it close to his ear and listen to what it was saying. Mūsā ﷺ did that and was astonished to hear it say:

سبحان من يراني ويسمع كلامي ويعلم مكاني ويذكرني ولا ينساني

'Pure is that Rabb Who is watching me, Who is listening to my speech,
Who knows where I am, and Who remembers me and does not forget me.'

Allāh ﷻ said, 'O Mūsā! I deliver its sustenance even in that secluded place. How am I going to forget you? Do not worry about it. I will cater for you also.' [43]

NEVER BE FEARFUL ABOUT RIZQ

People are always worried about rizq [sustenance]. Allāh ﷻ promises us in many places not to worry. Allāh ﷻ says in the Qur'ān:

وَمَا مِن دَابَّةٍ فِي الْأَرْضِ إِلَّا عَلَى اللَّهِ رِزْقُهَا وَيَعْلَمُ
مُسْتَقَرَّهَا وَمُسْتَوْدَعَهَا ۚ كُلٌّ فِي كِتَابٍ مُّبِينٍ ۞

---

[43] Tafsīr Mā'limul Irfān.

"The responsibility of sustaining the creatures on earth rests with Allāh. He knows the place where they will stay and the place they will be kept in trust. Everything is in the Clear Book." [44]

THE REPENTANCE OF A BANDIT

There was once a highway robber who along with his men ambushed a caravan of people and fled. They came upon a tree under which they decided to share their loot while sitting beneath it. They noticed a bird continuously flying away and returning to the tree. The leader of the bandits decided to climb the tree and observe what was going on. As he got up to the top, he saw a blind snake with its mouth open. This bird would go out to collect whatever insects it could carry and drop them into this snake's mouth. When he witnessed this scene, he immediately thought, 'O Allāh, this creature of yours, which causes harm to many, is in need, and you are providing for it in such a beautiful, caring manner. And here I am, from *ashraful makhlooqaat* and this is my state in looking for sustenance. O Allāh! Forgive me! Forgive me!' He dropped his sword asking forgiveness from Allāh. His companions also followed his lead in returning to Allāh ﷻ and they repented from their sins. They took the loot and returned it to the caravan apologising for their crime. As they walked on, they came across a town, wherein a man came to them and asked if a person by the name of so and so was amongst them. They replied in the affirmative, the man gave them a pouch full of wealth and said that a certain rich man was dying, and he appointed me to go and find a man with your name who would be coming this way. [45] This news may have come to him through a dream or a sign from Allāh ﷻ. This was the consequence of their repentance! Halāl sustenance reached them in this manner.

---

[44] Qur'ān 11:6.

[45] Fadhāil-e-Sadaqaat.

This is Allāh 🕮, the one who takes care of all affairs. Sometimes He may test us in the beginning, if we stay strong, He will then open doors for us from where we never imagined.

THE EFFORTS OF ĪMĀM BUKHĀRĪ 🕮

An example of this is to look at the life of Īmām Bukhārī 🕮. He came from a wealthy family and inherited a lot of wealth from his father. He spent all his wealth in acquiring Ahādīth. He went for Hajj with his elder brother, Ahmed and his mother. After Hajj, he decided to stay in Makkāh and Madīnāh to study under the Mashāikh of the Haramayn. His mother granted him permission to stay and left for home with Ahmed.

After attaining Ahādīth from the masters of Makkāh and Madīnāh, he travelled to Iraq, where he spent five years in Basra and many months in Kufa. He went back many a time to Kufa. He also visited Baghdad and Damascus along with other cities. During his journeys, his money finished and he continued in his quest for knowledge. From being quite affluent, he was now a pauper. He was worried and concerned. He did not want to beg to anyone for money, yet he had nothing but sweet leaves to live on. He would chew them to attain some taste. After a few more days like this, his condition deteriorated, but he stayed strong until finally Allāh 🕮 opened the doors for him. A random man came up to him and handed over a bag full of money. Īmām Bukhārī 🕮 thanked the man and knew this was from Allāh 🕮. [46]

WE HAVE TO PASS CERTAIN TESTS FIRST

Allāh 🕮 sometimes will test you before he opens up the doors. We realise Allāh 🕮 is the Rabb. He is the Controller and the Maintainer of everything. He is the one who gives out rizq. We should not run towards anyone but Allāh 🕮. Of course, we should work hard, study hard, earn halāl and do our day to day jobs,

---

[46] Fat'hul Baarī.

but we should always keep our sight towards Allāh ﷻ. Our jobs, our wages, our business do not feed us, our Rabb Who is the Khāliq, Maalik, and Raaziq is the One who looks after us. Remember Allāh ﷻ, do dhikr of Allāh ﷻ, worship Allāh ﷻ, and have hope in the mercy of Allāh ﷻ. Allāh ﷻ states in the Qur'ān:

$$\text{إِنَّ اللَّهَ يُحِبُّ الْمُتَوَكِّلِينَ ۝}$$

Allāh loves those who place their trust in Him. [47]

THE REASON WHY WE HAVE TO RECITE ALHAMDU SHAREEF 5 TIMES A DAY

We are instructed to recite الْحَمْدُ لِلَّهِ رَبِّ الْعَالَمِينَ many times a day to get the fact into our minds that Allāh ﷻ provides for us. He looks after us and the entire universe. He is the one who takes care of you and I. May Allāh ﷻ enable us to truly rely upon Him at all times. Āmīn!

THE HADĪTH OF TAWAKKUL

The Prophet ﷺ said:

$$\text{لو انكم توكلتم على الله حق توكله لرزقكم}$$
$$\text{كما يرزق الطير تغدو خماصا وتروح بطانا}$$

'If you relied upon Allāh ﷻ as He ought to be relied upon, then Allāh ﷻ would give you rizq like He gives to the birds, they leave in the morning with empty stomachs and come back in the evening satisfied.' [48]

---

[47] Qur'ān 3:159.
[48] Tirmīdhī, Mishkāt.

SHAYKH YŪNUS SAHIB'S TAWAKKUL

Shaykh Yūnus Sahib Dāmat Barakātuhum once said that he used to take wages from Madrasah Mazhāhirul Uloom. Then he thought to himself, let me forget all these wages, let me do tawakkul instead and rely totally upon Allāh ﷻ. He informed the office that after Ramadhān he will not take any wages. The staff tried to make Shaykh change his mind, but he was firm upon his intention. Shaykh said that at first it was very difficult and he had to borrow money off people to pay for medication and food etc. He said that one day he went into sajdāh in distress and said: 'O Allāh! These insects and birds are your creation and you feed them. I am also from your creation and in difficulty, please help me.' He says that since that day, Allāh ﷻ accepted my duā in such a way that Allāh ﷻ would provide without having to borrow.

OUR HADHRAT'S TAWAKKUL

Our respected Maulānā Yūsuf Motālā Dāmat Barakātuhum made such a big Darul Uloom. Māshā-Allāh, in 1973 he purchased the building; he then started formal teaching in 1975. Hadhrat Shaykh would frequently write letters of guidance to Hadhrat Yūsuf Motālā Sahib. He once wrote to Maulānā Yūsuf Sāhib to never take wages from the Madrasah. Our Hadhrat has never taken a penny from Darul Uloom. Initially, he had some difficulties. He would write to Hadhrat Shaykh about his condition. Sometimes he wouldn't have teabags to make a cup of tea for the guests. But in spite of this he wrote to Hadhrat Shaykh that I have no complaints towards Allāh ﷻ. I feel contentment in my heart. These are all documented in Hadhrat's letters. [49] Now we see Māshā-Allāh, how much Allāh ﷻ has assisted our Hadhrat. All these years have passed and he hasn't taken a penny, he has married twice and has had children and Allāh ﷻ continues to provide for him.

---

[49] Muhabbat Naame.

HADHRAT THĀNWĪ'S EXPLANATION OF TAWAKKUL

Hadhrat Thānwī ﷾ writes in one place that there are two types of tawakkul:

1. Tawakkul with means.
2. Tawakkul without means.

This second type is for the buzurgs and auliyaa of Allāh ﷻ. People like Hāfiz Patel ﷾. He had no source of income but Allāh ﷻ fed him and took him all around the world.

Maulānā Qāsim Nanotvi ﷾ once wrote a letter to Hājī Imdādullāh Muhājir Makkī ﷾ and said, 'Alhamdulillāh, the Darul Uloom is well established, my wage is five rupees a month. I feel like doing tawakkul by avoiding any remuneration from the institute. What is your opinion?' Hājī Sahib ﷾ wrote back saying, 'Do not stop yet. When the time comes when you do not need to take a second opinion regarding this matter, then you can stop taking it.' His asking his Shaykh's opinion was indicative that he had some hesitation in his heart. When a person reaches the highest stage, then he will totally rely upon Allāh ﷻ. This tawakkul without the means is for the true kaamileen.

This leaves us, the general public. For us, is tawakkul with means. Meaning, we use the means, we find a job, we find work and the money received is all due to Allāh ﷻ. Credit is due to Allāh ﷻ. We find halāl jobs, and do not look for jobs where one has to disgrace himself or overwork himself, as this will cause our bodies to be exhausted and lead to illnesses later in life. We should use the means and do tawakkul. We should get a job, work hard and also give time to Allāh ﷻ. We should also do dhikr, tilaawat, salāh etc.

BEING THANKFUL

'*Alhamdulillāh*' is the method of praising and thanking Allāh ﷻ because we have no other way of showing thanks other than through His praise.

The Prophet ﷺ said:

من لا يشكر الناس لا يشكر الله

36

'He who does not thank people, will not be thankful to Allāh.' [50]

In every situation we should strive to be thankful and grateful towards people for any act of kindness or favour. This will lead to the habit of being grateful to Allāh ﷻ and verbally praising Him at all times. We see this habit in the mashāikh, who are constantly uttering the praise of Allāh ﷻ.

ALLĀH LOVES THOSE WHO ARE GRATEFUL

Moreover, this is a habit which is beloved to Allāh ﷻ. It is narrated that: Anas bin. Mālik reported that Allāh's ﷻ Messenger ﷺ said:

ان الله ليرضى عن العبد ان ياكل الاكلة فيحمده

عليها او يشرب الشربة فيحمده عليها

'Allāh is pleased with His servant who says "Alhamdulillāh"
while taking a morsel of food and while drinking.' [51]

Of course, every effort should be made to say this with genuine gratefulness within the heart in order to please Allāh ﷻ.

ANOTHER HADĪTH FOR HAMD

It is also narrated that: Al-Mughira bin. Shu'ba ﷺ reported that Sa'd bin. 'Ubada ﷺ said, 'If I saw a man with my wife, I would strike him [behead him] with the blade of my sword.' This news reached Allāh's Messenger ﷺ who then said, 'You people are astonished at Sa'd's ghaira [protective jealousy]. By Allāh, I have more ghaira than he, and Allāh ﷻ has more ghaira than I. And Allāh ﷻ, because of His Ghaira, has made unlawful shameful deeds and sins [fornication etc] committed openly or secretly. And there is none who likes genuine reasoning more than Allāh ﷻ, and because of this, He sent the warners

---

[50] Abu Dāwūd: 4811, Tirmīdhī: 1954, 1955.
[51] Muslim: 2734 a.

and the givers of good news [so no excuse is left for kufr and shirk]. And there is none who likes to be praised more than Allāh 🕸, and for this reason, Allāh 🕸 has promised Paradise [so people do good, praise Him and attain the highest ranks.].' [52]

THE IMPORTANCE OF GHAIRA

Indeed, there is no one who has more ghaira [self-respect and protective jealousy] than Allāh 🕸 in regards to his servants, as stated in another Hadīth:

"O followers of Muhammad 🕋! By Allāh! There is none who has more ghaira [self-respect] than Allāh; so He has forbidden that His slaves, male or female, commit adultery. O followers of Muhammad 🕋! By Allāh! If you knew that which I know, you would laugh little and weep much." [53]

Therefore, it is imperative that we stay away from all indecency, lewdness and obscenity, so we can avoid displeasing of our Rabb.

PRAISING ALLĀH AT THE BEGINNING AND AT THE END OF A DUĀ

Returning to the previous Hadīth, we see that there is none who loves being praised more than Allāh 🕸, for which reason Allāh 🕸 grants Paradise, so we should strive to praise Him as much as possible. Even when we make duā, we should always begin and end with the praise and glorification of Allāh 🕸.

Fadalah bin `Ubaid 🕸 narrated: While the Messenger of Allāh 🕋 was seated, a man entered and performed salāh, and he said: 'O Allāh, forgive me, and have mercy upon me.' The Messenger of Allāh 🕋 said: 'You have rushed, O supplicator! When you perform salāh, then sit, then praise Allāh in a manner that He deserves, and send salāt upon me, then call upon Him.' He said: 'Then another man performed salāh after that, he praised Allāh and sent salāt upon

---

[52] Bukhārī: 7416, Muslim: 1499 a.
[53] Bukhārī: 1044, 5221.

the Prophet ﷺ. The Prophet ﷺ said to him: 'O supplicator! Supplicate, and you shall be answered.' [54]

PRAISING ALLĀH UNDER ALL CIRCUMSTANCES

It is for this reason we are taught within the masnoon prayers to praise Allāh ﷻ after eating or drinking, when wearing a garment, when exiting the bathroom, etc. In fact, according to another Hadīth, one of the names of this Ummah is al-Hammādūn, those who praise Allāh ﷻ most frequently: The first to be called to Paradise will be al-Hammādūn [those who praise Allāh ﷻ frequently], the ones who praise Allāh ﷻ upon every joy or woe. [55]

AL-HAMMĀDŪN

The reason for this name and status is that this Ummah praises Allāh ﷻ most often and more frequently than any other Ummah or nation that came before it. And this is all due to our noble Prophet Muhammad ﷺ, who praised Allāh ﷻ more than anyone else ever has or will. The Holy Prophet ﷺ praised Allāh ﷻ throughout his life and shall further praise Him on the Day of Judgement, as we learn from the narration below.

THE HADĪTH OF SHAFĀ'AT [INTERCESSION]

The Messenger of Allāh ﷺ said: Allāh ﷻ will gather the people on the Day of Resurrection and they will be concerned about it [and Ibn Ubaid said they will get a Divine inspiration about it] and will say: If we could seek intercession with our Rabb, we may be relieved from this predicament of ours. He [the Holy Prophet ﷺ] said: They will come to Adam ﷺ and say, Thou art Adam ﷺ, the father of mankind. Allāh ﷻ created thee with His own hand and breathed into thee of His Spirit and commanded the angels and they prostrated before thee.

---

[54] Tirmidhī: 3476.
[55] Abu Nu'aym: 6507, Hakim: 1784, Bazzar: 2928, Tabrānī: 12184.

So intercede for us with thy Rabb, that He may relieve us from this position of ours. He will say: I am not in a position to do this, and will recall his error, and will feel shy of his Rabb on account of that; [and will say] go to Noah ﷺ the first messenger [after me] sent by Allāh ﷺ. He [the Holy Prophet ﷺ] said: So they will come to Noah ﷺ. He will say: I am not in a position to do that for you, and recall his mistake which he committed, and will feel shy of his Rabb on account of that, [and will say]: Go to Ibrāhīm ﷺ whom Allāh ﷺ took for a close friend. They will come to Ibrahim ﷺ and he will say: I am not in a position to do that for you, and will recall his mistake that he had committed and will, therefore, feel shy of his Rabb on that account [and will say]: Go to Moses ﷺ with whom Allāh ﷺ conversed and conferred Torah upon him. He [the Holy Prophet ﷺ] said: So they will come to Moses ﷺ. He will say: I am not in a position to do that for you, and will recall his mistake that he had made and will feel shy of his Rabb on account of that [and will say]: Go to Jesus ﷺ, the Spirit of Allāh ﷺ and His word. He will say: I am not in a position to do that for you; you better go to Muhammad ﷺ, a servant whose former and later mistakes have all been forgiven.

He [the narrator] said: The Messenger of Allāh ﷺ observed: So they will come to me and I will ask the permission of my Rabb and it will be granted to me, and when I will see Him, I will fall down in prostration, and He [Allāh ﷺ] will leave me thus as long as He will wish, and then He will say: 'O Muhammad ﷺ, raise your head, say and you will be heard; ask and it will be granted; intercede and intercession will be accepted. Then I will raise my head and praise my Rabb with the praise which my Rabb will inspire in me. I shall then intercede, but a limit will be set for me. I will bring them out from the fire and make them enter Paradise [according to the limit].'

I shall return then and fall down in prostration and Allāh ﷺ will leave me [in that position] as long as He will wish to leave me, then it will be said: Rise, O Muhammad ﷺ, say and you will be heard; ask and it will be conferred; intercede and intercession will be granted. I will raise my head and praise my

<u>Rabb with praise that He will inspire in me</u>. I will then intercede and a limit will be set for me. I will bring them out of the fire [of Hell] and make them enter Paradise. He [the narrator] said: I do not remember whether he [the Holy Prophet ﷺ] said at the third time or at the fourth time: O my Rabb, none has been left in the Fire, but those restrained by the Holy Qur'ān, i.e. those who are eternally doomed. Ibn Ubaid said in a narration: Qatada observed: whose everlasting stay was imperative. [56]

This is one of the reasons why the Holy Prophet ﷺ was named Ahmed and Muhammad. Ahmed, meaning the one who praises the most from amongst all those who praise, and because he ﷺ praises Allāh ﷻ so much, he ﷺ is also named Muhammad, meaning the one who is praised often. And these are the names by which he ﷺ is most known: Ahmed, as he ﷺ was named by his ﷺ mother and known by the nations who came before us; and Muhammad, as he ﷺ was named by his ﷺ grandfather and is known to this Ummah.

PRAISING ALLĀH ﷻ FOR EVERY MORSEL

For all these reasons we should strive to praise Allāh ﷻ as much as possible. Not just after every meal but after every morsel, as Imām Ahmed bin Hanbal ﵀ once stated:

أكل وحمد خير من أكل صمت

'To eat and praise is better than to eat and remain silent.'

FEW ARE GRATEFUL

Allāh ﷻ commanded the Prophet Dāwūd ﵊ and his progeny saying:

اعْمَلُوا آلَ دَاوُودَ شُكْرًا ۚ وَقَلِيلٌ مِّنْ عِبَادِيَ الشَّكُورُ ۞

"Do good, O family of Dāwūd ﵊, in thankfulness.

---

[56] Muslim: 193 a.

Very few from My slaves are thankful." [57]

IBLĪS PROMOTES INGRATITUDE

The verse tells us that very few people are grateful to Allāh ﷻ. Indeed, it is one of Iblīs' primary goals to stop mankind from being grateful:

ثُمَّ لَآتِيَنَّهُم مِّن بَيْنِ أَيْدِيهِمْ وَمِنْ خَلْفِهِمْ وَعَنْ
أَيْمَانِهِمْ وَعَن شَمَائِلِهِمْ ۖ وَلَا تَجِدُ أَكْثَرَهُمْ شَاكِرِينَ ۝

*Then I will come upon them from their front and from their behind, and
from their right and from their left. You will not find most of them grateful.* [58]

Unfortunately, he has been successful in this, as Allāh ﷻ Himself confirms in the Noble Qur'ān:

وَلَقَدْ صَدَّقَ عَلَيْهِمْ إِبْلِيسُ ظَنَّهُ فَاتَّبَعُوهُ إِلَّا فَرِيقًا مِّنَ الْمُؤْمِنِينَ ۝

*Iblīs [Satan] has found his assessment true about them.
So they followed him, except a group of the believers.* [59]

EXAMPLES OF SHUKR OF THE PIOUS

Allāh ﷻ orders us in numerous places in the Qur'ān to be grateful to Him, and shows us how and why, through examples of His Prophets' ﷺ.

Allāh ﷻ says regarding Prophet Sulaimān ﷺ:

فَلَمَّا رَآهُ مُسْتَقِرًّا عِندَهُ قَالَ هَٰذَا مِن فَضْلِ رَبِّي لِيَبْلُوَنِي أَأَشْكُرُ أَمْ أَكْفُرُ ۖ

---

[57] Qur'ān 34:13.

[58] Qur'ān 7:17.

[59] Qur'ān 34:20.

$$\text{وَمَن شَكَرَ فَإِنَّمَا يَشْكُرُ لِنَفْسِهِ ۖ وَمَن كَفَرَ فَإِنَّ رَبِّي غَنِيٌّ كَرِيمٌ ۞}$$

"So when he saw it [the throne] well placed before him, he said, "This is by the grace of my Rabb, so that He may test me whether I am grateful or ungrateful. Whoever is grateful, is grateful for his own benefit, and whoever is ungrateful, then my Rabb is Need-Free, Bountiful." [60]

He says regarding Nūh ﷺ:

$$\text{إِنَّهُ كَانَ عَبْدًا شَكُورًا ۞}$$

"Surely he was an extremely grateful servant." [61]

And Allāh ﷻ promises us:

$$\text{وَإِذْ تَأَذَّنَ رَبُّكُمْ لَئِن شَكَرْتُمْ لَأَزِيدَنَّكُمْ ۖ وَلَئِن كَفَرْتُمْ إِنَّ عَذَابِي لَشَدِيدٌ ۞ وَقَالَ}$$

$$\text{مُوسَىٰ إِن تَكْفُرُوا أَنتُمْ وَمَن فِي الْأَرْضِ جَمِيعًا فَإِنَّ اللَّهَ لَغَنِيٌّ حَمِيدٌ ۞}$$

[Recall the time] when your Rabb declared, "If you express gratitude, I shall certainly give you more, and if you are ungrateful, then My punishment is severe." And Mūsā said, "If you and all those on earth become ungrateful, then Allāh is free of all needs, worthy of every praise." [62]

RECOUNT BLESSINGS OF ALLĀH ﷻ

We should always remain grateful to our Rabb, and recount all his favours upon us. The blessings with which he has bestowed us: our eyes, ears, and hands, our faces, hearts, and minds, etc. We have so much to be grateful for, if we but pay attention to His gifts. Ask the blind man how precious is the gift of

---

[60] Qur'ān 27:40.

[61] Qur'ān 17:3.

[62] Qur'ān 14:7-8.

one eye? Good health is a gift beyond price. What is more, being grateful only benefits ourselves and increases the gifts, whereas ungratefulness only harms us and our Rabb is free from needing our praises. We pray Allāh ﷻ gives us all the ability to be grateful.

SHUKR SHOULD BE DONE VERBALLY

In addition, this gratefulness within the heart should also be verbally spoken, as this is mentioned within the Glorious Qur'ān:

وَقَالُوا الْحَمْدُ لِلَّهِ الَّذِي أَذْهَبَ عَنَّا الْحَزَنَ ۖ إِنَّ رَبَّنَا لَغَفُورٌ شَكُورٌ ۞

الَّذِي أَحَلَّنَا دَارَ الْمُقَامَةِ مِن فَضْلِهِ لَا يَمَسُّنَا فِيهَا نَصَبٌ وَلَا يَمَسُّنَا فِيهَا لُغُوبٌ ۞

And they will say, "Praise be to Allāh who has removed all sorrow from us. Surely our Rabb is Most-Forgiving, Very-Appreciative. Who, out of His grace, has made us land at a home of eternal living where we are neither touched by weariness, nor are we touched by boredom." [63]

SHUKR OF THE DWELLERS OF JANNAH

وَقَالُوا الْحَمْدُ لِلَّهِ الَّذِي صَدَقَنَا وَعْدَهُ وَأَوْرَثَنَا الْأَرْضَ نَتَبَوَّأُ مِنَ

الْجَنَّةِ حَيْثُ نَشَاءُ ۖ فَنِعْمَ أَجْرُ الْعَامِلِينَ ۞ وَتَرَى الْمَلَائِكَةَ حَافِّينَ مِنْ حَوْلِ الْعَرْشِ

يُسَبِّحُونَ بِحَمْدِ رَبِّهِمْ ۖ وَقُضِيَ بَيْنَهُم بِالْحَقِّ وَقِيلَ الْحَمْدُ لِلَّهِ رَبِّ الْعَالَمِينَ ۞

And they will say, "Alhamdulillāh : Praise belongs to Allāh who made His promise come true for us, and made us inherit the territory, so as we can dwell anywhere we wish in Jannah [Paradise]. So, excellent is the reward of those who did [good] deeds. And you will see the angels ringed around the Throne proclaiming the purity of their

---

[63] Qur'ān 35:34-35.

Rabb, along with His praise, and matters will stand settled between them rightfully, and it will be said: "Alhamdulillāhi-rabbil'ālamīn : Praise belongs to Allāh, the Rabb of the worlds." [64]

And:

$$إِنَّ الَّذِينَ آمَنُوا وَعَمِلُوا الصَّالِحَاتِ يَهْدِيهِمْ رَبُّهُم بِإِيمَانِهِمْ ۖ تَجْرِي مِن تَحْتِهِمُ الْأَنْهَارُ$$

$$فِي جَنَّاتِ النَّعِيمِ ۞ دَعْوَاهُمْ فِيهَا سُبْحَانَكَ اللَّهُمَّ وَتَحِيَّتُهُمْ فِيهَا سَلَامٌ ۚ وَآخِرُ$$

$$دَعْوَاهُمْ أَنِ الْحَمْدُ لِلَّهِ رَبِّ الْعَالَمِينَ ۞$$

As for those who believe and do good deeds, their Rabb will guide them by virtue of their belief; rivers will be flowing beneath them in the Gardens of Bliss. Their call therein will be, "Pure are You, O Allāh" and their greeting therein will be Salām. And the end of their call will be, "Praise be to Allāh, the Rabb of all the worlds." [65]

These verses tell us that even in Paradise the tongues of the believers will be moist with their Rabb's remembrance and utter 'Alhamdulillāh' in eternal gratitude for their Rabb's favour.

Shaykh Yūnus Dāmat Barakātuhum once mentioned a Hadīth that Rasūlullāh ﷺ said: 'O Allāh! Please do this for me, and I will praise you.' That need was then fulfilled. He said: 'Alhamdulillāh!' The Sahāba, thinking he might have meant a lengthy praise asked, 'Ya Rasūlallāh! Your promise to Allāh?' He replied, 'I did say 'Alhamdulillāh'. This means that it can be enough when uttered with utmost concentration, and from the depth of the heart.

PRACTICAL SHUKR

Having covered the second type of shukr or gratitude, we come to the third type of shukr which is practical, by showing gratefulness through actions. To

---

[64] Qur'ān 39:74-75.
[65] Qur'ān 10:9-10.

practically show gratefulness for a gift, one should give a gift in return. Indeed, one should be more frequent in the giving of gifts than in receiving them, and no gift should be deemed too small or too insignificant to give to a neighbour, a relative or a friend. It is a practice, especially in Ramadhān, when food is made for iftār that some food is sent to the neighbours or to the Masjid for the opening of fasts. This practice is encouraged in Ahādīth.

SHUKR OF ONE'S NEIGHBOURS

Abu Dharr ﷺ reported: My Khaleel [i.e. close friend] [the Messenger of Allāh ﷺ] advised me saying, "Whenever you prepare a broth, put plenty of water in it, and give some to your neighbours and give them with courtesy." [66]

And:

Abu Hurairah ﷺ reported: The Messenger of Allāh ﷺ said, "O Muslim women! None of you should consider insignificant [a gift] to give to her neighbour even if it is [a gift of] the hoof of a sheep." [67]

And:

Do you know what the right of a neighbour is? [It is] To help him if he seeks your help; to lend to him if he seeks a loan; to help him regain something lost; to visit him when he is sick; to congratulate him when some good comes to him; to console him when he is struck with misfortune; to follow his funeral after his death; not to build an extension overlooking him, which would stop the breeze reaching him, [without his permission], not to throw your litter in his garden and to gift him some of the fruit you buy for yourself. [68]

---

[66] Muslim: 2625 b, al-Adab al-Mufrad: 114, Riyādh as-Salihīn: 304.
[67] Bukhārī: 2566, 6017, Muslim: 1030.
[68] Jami' al-ulūm wal-hikam: pg.351.

PRACTICAL SHUKR OF ALLĀH ﷻ

Obviously, we cannot give gifts of food and such to our Rabb, Allāh ﷻ. However, what we can do to show our practical gratefulness is to do acts of optional worship. To perform optional salāh, Hajj, give sadaqah, fast, and recite the Holy Qur'ān. Moreover, these optional prayers will cover our shortcomings in the fulfilling of our compulsory worship, and also enable us to gain reward by showing our devotion. It is narrated that Umm Habibah ﵂ says: The Prophet ﷺ said:

"Whoever prays twelve rak'āhs during the day and night, a house will be built for him in Paradise." [69] [Two before fajr, four before zuhr and two after zuhr, two after maghrib, and two after ishā]."

SUNNATE MUAKKADAH ARE A FORM OF SHUKR

Some people are of the opinion that you shouldn't pray the sunnah prayers when in a state of travelling, going as far as to say that it is a sin. Some people refrain from praying sunnah in Minā, Arafāt and Muzdalifā during Hajj. We had one such lady from Al-Huda International who would get angry at the ladies for praying sunnah. She wouldn't pray and she wouldn't let other pray. This is absolutely wrong. There are two states within travelling: firstly, there is the time when you are actually in a state of travel from one place to the next, such as at an airport or train station or service station, or on the actual plane or train, and travelling; secondly, when you are far from home but staying at a place for a while, such as staying at a friend's house for a few days or attending an event. In the second case, it is actually recommended to continue praying sunnah and optional prayers so as to stay in the habit of the sunnah. We should strive to perform more acts of worship rather than less and pray

---

[69] Nasa'i: 1804, 1810.

optional prayers as well, such as salāhtut tasbīh, as they carry great reward and strengthen our will to pray the compulsory prayers.

EVIDENCE FOR PERFORMING SUNNAH IN SAFR

There is a Hadīth in Sahīh Bukhārī which states that Rasūlullāh ﷺ and the caravan of Sahāba overslept and fajr became Qadhā. They performed the two sunnah first and then the Qadhā.

THE METHOD OF SALĀHTUT-TASBĪH

We now put forward the Hadīth of salāhtut tasbīh for those who would be interested to learn and practice.

Abū Rafi ﷺ narrates that:

Allāh's Messenger ﷺ said to Al-Abbās ﷺ: "O uncle! Shall I not give to you, shall I not present to you, [and] shall I not benefit you?" He said: "Of course, O Messenger of Allāh ﷺ!" He said: "O uncle! Pray four rak'āh, reciting in each rak'āh Fātihatil-Kitāb and a sūrah. When you are finished with your recitation then say: 'Subhānallāh, Wal-hamdulillāh, Wa Lā Ilāhā illallāhū, Wallāhu Akbar.' [Glorious is Allāh, all praise is due to Allāh, and there is none worthy of worship except Allāh, and Allāh is the Greatest]. Say this fifteen times before you bow. Then bow and say it ten times, then raise your head and say it ten times. Then prostrate and say it ten times, then sit and say it ten times. Then prostrate [the second time] and say it ten times. Then raise your head and say it ten times before standing. That is seventy-five in every rak'āh, which is three-hundred in four rak'āh. If your sins were like a heap of sand then Allāh would forgive you." He said: "O Messenger of Allāh! Who is able to pray that every day?" He said: "If you cannot pray it every day then pray it every Friday, and if you are not able to pray it every Friday then pray it every month." And he did not stop saying that until he said: "Then pray it every year." [70]

Hadhrat Shaykhul Ḥadīth Muhammad Zakariyyā ﷺ would go early for the Jumu'ah prayer and pray Salāhtut tasbīh consistently throughout his life. In Ramadhān, they would be punctual with salāhtut tasbīh alongside their other daily routines. The blessed mother of our own shaykh, Hadhrat Yūsuf Motālā [May Allāh ﷺ preserve them and continue to bless us with his presence], would pray salāhtut tasbīh daily alongside a routine of reciting five or six pārās of the Qur'ān. Those who are fulltime parents and remain at home should pay special consideration to this form of worship and strive to make it part of their daily life. We should all strive to increase our acts of worship as this is how we show our gratefulness to Allāh ﷺ through action.

THE MEANING OF 'LILLĀHĪ'

Having discussed hamd and gratefulness in all its forms, we come to the second half of the phrase 'Alhamdulillāh'. The words 'lillāh' translates as 'for Allāh', and mean that all gratefulness and praise is exclusively for Allāh. At this point, an argument could be put forth that we praise others as well, such as when we see skilled craftsmen, artisans, and professionals achieve something outstanding or remarkable. This, however, can be dismissed because we can either praise someone directly by praising their being or indirectly by praising something attributed to that person. It can be reasoned, as an example, that praising a vehicle for its handling and performance is in fact praise of the engineers who designed and crafted it; which is actually praising the minds that manufactured the product; which is in reality praise of Him who created these minds. It is for this reason that we should always have our hearts and minds attached to Allāh ﷺ, who is the real Creator, and whenever we see

---

[70] Tirmīdhī: 482, Abu Dāwūd: 1297.

something good we should say, 'Alhamdūlillāh MashāAllāh, lā qūwwata illā billāh.

THE ROOT OF THE NAME 'ALLĀH'

Having discussed the meaning of *hamd* and its implications, the exegete Baidhāwī ﷻ begins a discussion on the etymology of the name 'Allāh' [الله] within the phrase, '*alhamdulillāh*'.

The first question that arises is whether 'Allāh' is an Arabic or non-Arabic name. Some scholars have argued that the word is Syrian/Aramaic in origin and was assimilated into Arabic, however, the majority of scholars are of the opinion that it is of Arabic origin.

The name 'Allāh' is derived from the word al-*Ilāh*, which has its etymological roots in *walāhā, yalīhū*, and was altered from *wilāh* into ilāh. *Walāhā, yalīhū, walhan* carries the meaning, 'to be perplexed' or 'to be concerned/troubled' by something or someone. The word *wilāh* means 'that being who constantly perplexes, and confounds, amazes and astounds.' From *wilāh*, the word became ilāh and was later transformed into the word 'Allāh' via the process of *tā'leel*. Allāh, then, is the proper noun applied to that Being who is Wājibul Wūjood [i.e. who exists necessarily], by Himself, and comprises all excellent qualities and the attributes of perfection and is free of all faults and imperfections. This definition is supported by the following verses:

$$\text{قُلْ هُوَ اللَّهُ أَحَدٌ ۞ اللَّهُ الصَّمَدُ ۞}$$

$$\text{لَمْ يَلِدْ وَلَمْ يُولَدْ ۞ وَلَمْ يَكُن لَّهُ كُفُوًا أَحَدٌ ۞}$$

Say, "[The truth is that] Allāh is One. Allāh is Besought of All, needing none. He neither begot anyone, nor was he begotten. And equal to Him has never been any one." [71]

---

[71] Qur'ān 112:1-4.

THE ASMĀE HUSNĀ

Allāh is the *ism-dhāt* [noun of being], there are however other adjectival nouns, which describe Allāh's specific qualities and attributes. These adjectival nouns are known as the *Asmā al-Husnā*, i.e. the Beautiful Names, as stated in the verse:

وَلِلَّهِ الْأَسْمَاءُ الْحُسْنَىٰ فَادْعُوهُ بِهَا ۖ وَذَرُوا الَّذِينَ يُلْحِدُونَ فِي أَسْمَائِهِ ۚ سَيُجْزَوْنَ مَا كَانُوا يَعْمَلُونَ ۞

For Allāh there are the most beautiful names. So, call Him by them, and leave those who deviate in [the matter of] His names. They shall be recompensed for what they have been doing. [72]

And the verse:

قُلِ ادْعُوا اللَّهَ أَوِ ادْعُوا الرَّحْمَٰنَ ۖ أَيًّا مَّا تَدْعُوا فَلَهُ الْأَسْمَاءُ الْحُسْنَىٰ ۚ

Say, "Call [Him by the name of] Allāh or Ar-Rahmān, in whichever way you call, His are the Best Names" [73]

Some of the Beautiful Names are mentioned in the Qur'ān, as in the verses:

هُوَ اللَّهُ الَّذِي لَا إِلَٰهَ إِلَّا هُوَ ۖ عَالِمُ الْغَيْبِ وَالشَّهَادَةِ ۖ هُوَ الرَّحْمَٰنُ الرَّحِيمُ ۞ هُوَ اللَّهُ الَّذِي لَا إِلَٰهَ إِلَّا هُوَ الْمَلِكُ الْقُدُّوسُ السَّلَامُ الْمُؤْمِنُ الْمُهَيْمِنُ الْعَزِيزُ الْجَبَّارُ الْمُتَكَبِّرُ ۚ سُبْحَانَ اللَّهِ عَمَّا يُشْرِكُونَ ۞ هُوَ اللَّهُ الْخَالِقُ الْبَارِئُ الْمُصَوِّرُ ۖ لَهُ الْأَسْمَاءُ الْحُسْنَىٰ ۚ يُسَبِّحُ لَهُ مَا فِي السَّمَاوَاتِ وَالْأَرْضِ ۖ وَهُوَ الْعَزِيزُ الْحَكِيمُ ۞

---

[72] Qur'ān 7:180.
[73] Qur'ān 17:110.

He is Allāh, besides whom there is no god, the Knower of the unseen and the seen.
He is All-Merciful, Very-Merciful. He is Allāh, besides whom there is no god, the
Sovereign, the Supreme-In-Holiness, the Safe [from all defects], the Giver-Of-Peace,
the Guardian, the All-Mighty, the All-Repairer, [and] the Sublime. Pure is Allāh from
what they associate with Him. He is Allāh, the Creator, the Inventor, [and] the Shaper.
His are the Most Beautiful Names. His purity is proclaimed by all that are in the
heavens and in the earth, and He is the All-Mighty, the All-Wise. [74]

As regards to the number of the Beautiful Names, these are the ninety nine names of Allāh ﷻ, which are mentioned in the Hadīth. The Prophet ﷺ has stated:

Allāh has ninety-nine names, i.e. one-hundred minus one,
and whoever covers them [i.e. memorises them] will go to Paradise. [75]

Moreover, in another Hadīth, the Prophet ﷺ recounts the entirety of the ninety names which are mentioned, stating:

Indeed, Allāh has ninety-nine names, one hundred less one, and whosoever counts them shall enter Paradise. He is Allāh, the one beside whom there is none worthy of worship [*Allāhu Lā Ilāha Illā Huwa*], the Most Merciful [to the creation] [*Ar-Raḥmān*], the Most Beneficent [to the believers] [*Ar-Raḥīm*], the King [Al-Malik], the Free of Deficiencies [Al-*Quddūs*], the Granter of Safety [As-Salām], the Granter of Security [Al-*Mu'min*], the Watcher [Al-*Muhaimin*], the Mighty [Al-`Azīz], the Compeller [Al-*Jabbār*], the Supreme [Al-*Mutakabbir*], the Creator [Al-*Khāliq*], the Originator [Al-*Bāri'*], the Fashioner [Al-*Muṣawwir*], the Pardoner [Al-*Ghaffār*], the Overwhelming [Al-*Qahhār*], the Giving [Al-*Wahhāb*], the Provider [Ar-*Razzāq*], the Opener [Al-*Fattāḥ*], the Knowing [Al-`Alīm], the Taker [Al-*Qābiḍ*], the Giver [Al-*Bāsiṭ*], the One Who Abases [Al-

---

Khāfiḍ], the Exalter [Ar-*Rāfi`*], the One who grants honour [Al-*Mu`izz*], the One who humiliates [Al-*Mudhil*], the Hearing [As-Samī`], the Seeing [Al-Baṣīr], the Judge [Al-Ḥakam], the Just [Al-`Adl], the Kind [Al-Laṭīf], the Aware [Al-Khabīr], the Forbearing [Al-Ḥalīm], the Magnificent [Al-`Aẓīm], the Oft-Forgiving [Al-*Ghafūr*], the Grateful [Ash-Shakūr], the Most High [Al-`Aliyy], the Great [Al-*Kabīr*], the Guardian [Al-*Ḥafīẓ*], the Powerful [Al-Muqīt], the Reckoner [Al-Ḥasīb], the Glorious [Al-*Jalīl*], the Generous [Al-*Karīm*], the Watcher [Ar-Raqīb], the Responder [Al-Mujīb], the Liberal Giver [Al-*Wāsi`*], the Wise [Al-Ḥakīm], the Loving [Al-Wadūd], the Majestic [Al-Majīd], the Reviver [Al-Bā`*ith*], the Witness [Ash-Shahīd], the Truth [Al-Ḥaqq], the Guarantor [Al-Wakīl], the *Strong* [Al-*Qawiyy*], the Firm [Al-Matīn], the One Who Aids [Al-Waliyy], the Praiseworthy [Al-Ḥamīd], the Encompasser [Al-Muḥṣi], the One Who Begins things [Al-Mubdi'], the One Who brings things back [Al-Mu`īd], the One Who gives life [Al-Muḥyi], the One Who causes death [Al-Mumīt], the Living [Al-Ḥayyu], the Self-Sufficient [Al-Qayyūm], the One Who brings into existence [Al-Wājid], the Illustrious [Al-Mājid], the One [Al-Wāḥid], the Master [Aṣ-Ṣamad], the Able [Al-*Qādir*], the Powerful [Al-Muqtadir], the One who brings forward [Al-*Muqaddim*], the One who puts behind [Al-Mu'akhkhir], the First [Al-Awwal], the Last [Al-*Ākhir*], the Apparent [Aẓ-Ẓāhir], the Inner [Al-Bāṭin], the Owner [Al-Wāli], the Exalted [Al-*Muta`āli*], the Doer of Good [Al-*Barr*], the Acceptor of repentance [At-Tawwāb], the Avenger [Al-*Muntaqim*], the Pardoning [Al-`*Afuww*], the Kind [Ar-*Raūf*], the Owner of Dominion [*Mālikul-Mulk*], the Possessor of Glory and Generosity [*Dhul Jalāli wal Ikrām*], the One who does justice [Al-Muqsiṭ], the Gatherer [Al-Jāmi`], the Rich [Al-*Ghaniyy*], the Enricher [Al-*Mughni*], the Preventer [Al-*Māni`*], the One who can harm [Aḍ-*Ḍhārr*], the One who benefits [An-*Nāfi`*], the Light [An-*Nūr*], the Guide [Al-*Hādi*], the Originator [Al-*Badī`*], the Lasting [Al-*Bāqi*], the Inheritor [Al-*Wārith*], the Guide [Ar-*Rashīd*], the Tolerant [Aṣ-Ṣabūr]. [76]

---

[76] Jami'at-Tirmīdhī: 3507.

These are all adjectival nouns of Allāh 🌸, which state His attributes whereas Allāh is the noun of being. It is desired that Allāh 🌸 be called upon by these names within our prayers as was revealed in the aforementioned verses. In fact, some mashāikh would make their disciples recite a litany of the ninety nine Beautiful Names.

SAHL TUSTURĪ'S 🌸 EXPERIENCE

Sahl bin Abdullāh al-Tusturī 🌸 would recite each name and have his disciple repeat it after him, until he felt one of the names affecting his disciple's heart more than the others, in which case that name would become the disciple's litany as he considered the cure to that person's spiritual ailments to be within that name. If none of the names affected the person, Sahl bin Abdullāh al-Tusturī 🌸 would not take him as a disciple and ask him to take his pledge with someone else.

READING YĀ QAWĪYYŪ AND YĀ NŪRŪ AFTER SALĀH

The Beautiful Names are indeed a cure to many spiritual ailments as well as a means of having prayers accepted. For example, Yā Qawīyyū recited eleven times after salāh is a proven cure for weakness of memory, and similarly reciting Yā Nūrū is a cure for problems with sight. My own shaykh, the respected Hadhrat Yūsuf Motāla Dāmat Barakātuhum, once instructed me to recite a litany of Yā Qayyūmū 125,000 times and thereafter Yā Rahīmū 125,000 times, during the period of Hajj. Once this was completed, he gave me permission to use these blessed names as a form of *ruqyah* or treatment, as the effect of these names can be much more. This is a form of *tarbiyat* [training] by the *mashāikh* through the use of the ninety nine names of Allāh 🌸. Furthermore, this use of the Beautiful Names as a litany cannot be construed as an innovation, as it is supported by the Qur'ānic statement:

$$\text{وَلِلَّهِ الْأَسْمَاءُ الْحُسْنَىٰ فَادْعُوهُ بِهَا ۞}$$

'For Allāh there are the most beautiful names. So, call upon Him by them'. [77]

Shaykh Yūnus Sahib said: 'This practice may not be sunnah in itself, however, Ilaaj [searching for cure] is sunnah, so to read it with the intention of cure will be following the sunnah.'

A Story of Imām Jā'far Sādiq

Laith bin Saa'd says: 'In the year 113 A.H., I went to Makkāh on foot to perform Hajj. One day at the time of Asr salāh, I climbed onto Mount Abu Qubais where I saw a man sitting and making duā. So many times did he utter the words, 'Yā Rabb' [O Lord] that it took his breath away. Then he started uttering, 'Yā Rabbaah' [O my dear Lord]. He did this until he was out of breath, then he went over to saying, 'Yā Hay, Yā Hay' [O, the Living One]. Then, 'Yā Rahmān' [O, Beneficent One], and then, 'Yā Arhamar Rāhimeen', [O Most Merciful of all Merciful Ones].'

Then he said, 'O Allāh, I desire to eat grapes; so grant me of that; and my clothes are worn out too.'

Laith continues: 'I swear by Allāh! The words had hardly left his lips when I saw a basket of grapes by his side, and two cloaks. This astonished me for there were no grapes to be seen in the whole of Makkāh. He was about to start eating the grapes when I said to him, 'I have a right to be your partner in eating that.' He replied, 'How is that?' I said, 'When you prayed, I said Āmīn Āmīn.' He replied, 'Very well, come and eat but do not take anything of it with you.'

I approached and ate with him. It had a delicious taste as I had never tasted before in my life. It was such a wonderful type of grape without seeds. I ate myself to the full, yet the basket remained as full as ever.

Then he said, 'Take any one of those two cloaks that you like.' I replied that I was not in need of clothing.

[77] Qur'ān 7:180.

Then he asked me to excuse him while he dressed himself. I moved away. He wrapped the one piece of cloth around his lower body like a lūngī, and the other piece over his upper body. Then being clothed, he descended the mountain while I followed him.

When he came between Safā and Marwā, a beggar said to him: 'O son of Rasūlullāh ﷺ, give these clothes to me. May Allāh grant you a pair from Paradise.' He gave the clothes to the beggar. Hearing the beggars words, I asked him, 'Who is this generous person?' He replied, 'He is Īmām Jā'far as-Sādiq ﷺ.'

Then I turned to listen to some of his words but by then he had gone and was nowhere to be seen. [78]

Allāh ﷻ is still the same Allāh ﷻ who heard the prayer of Īmām Jā'far as-Sādiq ﷺ, it is only ourselves who have changed and it is we who need some rectification.

DHIKR WITH ISME ZAAT

Thus far we have considered the permissibility, benefits and desirability of repeating the adjectival nouns of Allāh ﷻ. Now it is left to look into the repetition and litany of the isme zaat, i.e. Allāh. Again it is entirely permissible, desirable and recommended to repeat the name Allāh ﷻ, as this is the name He has chosen for Himself. Indeed, He has commanded us to make remembrance of Him by His name in various verses:

$$\text{وَاذْكُرِ اسْمَ رَبِّكَ وَتَبَتَّلْ إِلَيْهِ تَبْتِيلًا ۝}$$

$$\text{رَّبُّ الْمَشْرِقِ وَالْمَغْرِبِ لَا إِلَهَ إِلَّا هُوَ فَاتَّخِذْهُ وَكِيلًا ۝}$$

And invoke the name of your Rabb, and devote yourself to Him with exclusive devotion. He is the Rabb of the East and the West; there is no god but Him; so take Him for [your] Guardian. [79]

---

[78] Virtues of Hajj by Maulānā Mohammad Zakarīyā Khāndelwī, pg.272-273.
[79] Qur'ān 73:8-9.

And:

$$وَاذْكُرِ اسْمَ رَبِّكَ بُكْرَةً وَأَصِيلًا ۞$$

$$وَمِنَ اللَّيْلِ فَاسْجُدْ لَهُ وَسَبِّحْهُ لَيْلًا طَوِيلًا ۞$$

And pronounce the name of Allāh morning and evening. And in some parts of the night prostrate yourself before Him, and pronounce His purity for long times at night. [80]

And also:

$$قَدْ أَفْلَحَ مَن تَزَكَّىٰ ۞ وَذَكَرَ اسْمَ رَبِّهِ فَصَلَّىٰ ۞$$

Success is surely achieved by him who purifies himself, and pronounces the name of his Rabb, then offers prayer. [81]

As the proper name for the Supreme Being is Allāh ﷻ, these verses denote that the dhikr, litany and repetition of the name of Allāh ﷻ is not just permissible, but recommended too, and a source of strength for the rooh. The Qur'ān states:

$$الَّذِينَ آمَنُوا وَتَطْمَئِنُّ قُلُوبُهُم بِذِكْرِ اللَّهِ ۗ أَلَا بِذِكْرِ اللَّهِ تَطْمَئِنُّ الْقُلُوبُ ۞$$

$$الَّذِينَ آمَنُوا وَعَمِلُوا الصَّالِحَاتِ طُوبَىٰ لَهُمْ وَحُسْنُ مَآبٍ ۞$$

. . . The ones who believe and their hearts are peaceful with the remembrance of Allāh. Listen! The hearts find peace only in the remembrance of Allāh. Those who believe and do good deeds, for them there is the bliss and a good place to return. [82]

---

[80] Qur'ān 76:25-26.

[81] Qur'ān 87: 14-15.

[82] Qur'ān 13:28-29.

The heart and soul can only gain peace through the remembrance of Allāh ﷻ, as it is this remembrance which nourishes them. Music and all other arts can only nourish the carnal self, as they are all linked to the carnal self's desires, and after a brief seating, they will leave a person restless and distraught again. It is the nourishment of the heart and soul that can bring true contentment and inner peace. Only remembrance of His name can provide serenity and rest. True harmony is in the litanies of Allāh, Allāh. The *mashāikh* urge their disciples to perform litanies of His divine name, as this creates a constant awareness of Allāh ﷻ.

EVIDENCE FOR DHIKR MAJLIS

Although the Sahābah ﷺ did not do dhikr in the exact format which is prescribed by the various orders of *tazkiyah* and *tasawwuf*, the roots of these forms of dhikr can be found within the actions of the Sahābā ﷺ and the Holy Prophet ﷺ, as is reported by Abū Sa'id Khudrī ﷺ who states that:

> Mu'āwiya ﷺ went to a circle in the mosque and said: What makes you sit here? They said: We are sitting here in order to remember Allāh. He said: I adjure you by Allāh [to tell me whether you are sitting here for this very purpose]? They said: By Allāh, we are sitting here for this very purpose. Thereupon, he said: I have not demanded you to take an oath, because of any suspicion about you and none of my rank in the eye of Allāh's Messenger ﷺ is the narrator of so few ahādīth as I am. The fact is that Allāh's Messenger ﷺ went out to the circle of his Companions ﷺ and said: What makes you sit? They said: We are sitting here in order to remember Allāh and to praise Him for He guided us to the path of Islām and He conferred favours upon us. Thereupon he ﷺ adjured by Allāh and asked if that only was the purpose of their sitting there. They said: By Allāh, we are not sitting here but for this very purpose, whereupon he [the Messenger ﷺ] said: I am not asking you to take an oath because of any allegation against you but for the fact that

Gabriel came to me and he informed me that Allāh, the Exalted and Glorious, was talking to the angels about your magnificence. [83]

Also, Anas bin Mālik 🅐 narrated that the Messenger of Allāh 🅐 said:

"When you pass by the gardens of Paradise, then feast." They [the Companions 🅐] asked: "And what are the gardens of Paradise?" He 🅐 replied: "The circles of remembrance." [84]

Allāmā Suyūtī 🅐 narrates that during the caliphate of Umar bin Khattāb 🅐 a gathering of Muslims would constantly be engaged in the dhikr of Allāh 🅐 within the mosque. Whenever Umar 🅐 would hear their voices waning and growing quiet, he 🅐 would encourage them to raise their voices in dhikr. Umar 🅐 himself would recite the Qur'ān aloud to such an extent that his voice was heard in the farthest parts of the Masjid. It is from the practice of Allāh's Messenger 🅐 and his Sahāba 🅐, the *mashāikh* have taken the practice of dhikr. The dhikr of 'Allāh, Allāh' is necessary for the existence of all things, as the Hadīth on the authority of Anas 🅐 states that the Messenger of Allāh 🅐 said:

The Hour [Resurrection} will not occur until there
is no one on the earth saying: 'Allāh, Allāh.' [85]

THE PLEASURE OF REPEATING ALLĀH'S NAME

What is more, there is no pleasure greater than the remembrance of Allāh 🅐, as Rūmī 🅐 would say:

---

[83] Sahīh Muslim: 2701.

[84] Jami'at-Tirmīdhī: 3510.

[85] Sahīh Muslim: 148 b.

الله الله این چه شیرین است نام شیر و شکر می شود جانم تمام

Allāh, Allāh! How sweet a name it is! My entire being is made sweet because of it!

The eminent shaykh, Shah Abdul Qādir Raipūrī ﷽ would sit in a state of meditation while his disciples sat around him and make dhikr. Occasionally, he would raise his head and look toward them and recite:

اللہ اللہ ہے تو گویا جان ہے۔ ورنہ یار و حجان بھی بے جان ہے۔

Only with the dhikr of Allāh, Allāh is there life, otherwise even life becomes lifeless.

A final point worth mentioning here is that while Allāh ﷻ is the Arabic name for the Supreme Being, it is recommended that it be used in all situations. However, that is not to say other names cannot be used when speaking other languages. It is also permissible to use other names in other languages such as God in English, or Khudā in Persian, as these are words used to denote the Supreme Being and will not be considered a form of shirk [polytheism].

VERSE 2

الرَّحْمٰنِ الرَّحِيمِ ﴿٢﴾

The Most Beneficent, the Most Merciful

Rahmān and Rahīm are very pertinent qualities of Allāh ﷻ, which is why they have been brought into bismillāh. Allāh ﷻ could have used any other of his 99+ names, but chose to use Al-Rahmān and Al-Rahīm. Allāh ﷻ also uses these qualities to describe Himself in the concluding verses of Sūrah Hashr:

هُوَ اللَّهُ الَّذِي لَا إِلَهَ إِلَّا هُوَ عَالِمُ الْغَيْبِ وَالشَّهَادَةِ هُوَ الرَّحْمَنُ الرَّحِيمُ ۞

He is Allāh, there is no Ilaah but He. He is the Knower of the unseen and the seen. He is the Most Compassionate, the Most Merciful. [86]

---

[86] Qur'ān 59:22.

He also starts Sūrah Rahmān using the same. Repeating the name in various places shows His love for this word 'Rahmān'.

In one Hadīth, the Messenger ﷺ says:

أَحَبُّ الأَسْمَاءِ إِلَى اللَّهِ عَزَّ وَجَلَّ عَبْدُ اللَّهِ وَعَبْدُ الرَّحْمَنِ

'The most beloved names to Allāh are Abdullāh and Abdur-Rahmān.' [87]

We should name our children with these names because Allāh ﷻ likes them very much.

THE MEANING OF RAHMAH

Rahmān is derived from the word Rahmah. Rahmah is the feeling in your heart, meaning, to be merciful or benevolent to somebody after considering their state or condition. It is a natural reaction that shakes a man when seeing a poor person, an injured person, an orphan, or a sick person. Every person has rahmah in them – some more than others, yet this emotion is only found in creatures.

A question arises here that if it is a human inner-emotion [infi'āl], how can Allāh ﷻ also experience this rahmah? The salaf would not delve into such questions. They would simply say, "أمروها كما جاءت" – 'Let these nūsoos [wordings] pass by as they have come.' i.e We read them, we believe in them, and we leave their details to Allāh ﷻ. We know He is Rahmān and Rahīm. We cannot describe the haqeeqat and reality of His Rahmah. Allāh ﷻ knows best. However, the later scholars mentioned some meaning to such wordings. They did not say for certain that this is the intended meaning. They merely said that there is the possibility that our understanding of what Allāh is saying, should be this.

---

[87] Ibn Mājah: 3728; Nasa'ī: 3565; Abu Dāwūd: 4949; Tirmīdhī: 3067; Al-Adab Al-Mufrad: 814.

The above query has been explained by Qādhī Baidhāwī ﷺ in his tafsīr. He explains it by first describing the emotions of humans, and what they go through when experiencing such emotions; for example, when angry, a person's face will turn red, his cheeks will puff, he will breathe heavily and his veins will swell, due to the pumping of the blood. If we then say that Allāh ﷻ becoming angry would necessitate all these reactions, then this is inappropriate. However, it can be explained that every action of emotion has a beginning and an end. The start point is the initial emotion and the end point is the consequence or outcome of such a reaction.

Let us use the example of rahmah; the initial stage would be the emotion kicking in and hitting a nerve in his heart, the final stage would be giving the poor some money, treating the sick, looking after them and taking them to the hospital.

If a person is angry, the consequences would be that he would lash out; he would hit whoever is making him angry and would want to cause him harm.

So Qādhī Baidhāwī ﷺ states that the end point and consequence of the mercy of Allāh ﷻ is that Allāh ﷻ blesses him, showers His favours upon him, makes him His beloved, elevates his status and grants him acceptance amongst the people. And when Allāh ﷻ becomes angry with somebody, he punishes him, He distances the person from His mercy, etc. So with regards to Allāh ﷻ, the final consequence is what is intended, not the initial stages

BE MERCIFUL TO THE CREATION

Allāh ﷻ is Rahmān and Rahīm and has only created everything due to His infinite mercy. Allāh ﷻ wanted to bless us and shower His favours upon us so that we turn back towards Him, worship Him and obey Him, so that again He can show us mercy and grant us entry into His Jannah, so that we are able to enjoy its rewards. This is why Rasūlullāh ﷺ says in a Hadīth:

الراحمون يرحمهم الرحمن تبارك وتعالى ارحموا من في الارض يرحمكم من في السماء .

The Compassionate One has mercy on those who themselves are merciful. Show mercy to those on the earth, He Who is in the heavens will show mercy to you. [88]

'*In the heavens*' can be left to the meaning intended by Allāh ﷻ and his Rasūl, as the salafs would. It could mean 'the one whose commands are sent down from the heavens'. It could also mean 'the angels who are in the heaven' will bring mercy to him.

A SAYING OF SHAYKH YŪNUS SAHIB

Our teacher, Shaykh Yūnus Jaunpūrī Dāmat Barakātuhum, says that this Hadīth is what the teacher recites to his students first, before continuing with the other Ahādīth. The reason he mentions it, is that the initiation of the universe happened due to rahmah [mercy]. So a teacher should also initiate his teaching of Hadīth with the Hadīth of Rahmah. He should remind himself, as well as the student to hold onto mercy, gentleness and kindness.

It was only due to the mercy of Allāh ﷻ, that he created the heavens and the earth. This is why the Prophet ﷺ said:

'When Allāh created the creation, He wrote above His Throne:

$$\text{إِنَّ رَحْمَتِي سَبَقَتْ غَضَبِي}$$

My mercy precedes my wrath. [89]

ALLĀH'S MERCY SUPERSEDES HIS WRATH

Allāh ﷻ displays His Mercy more than His Anger, and it's true that Allāh's ﷻ mercy is forever with us, and seldom does He display his anger. Calamities, problems, and accidents occur rarely. Floods, earthquakes, and Tsunamis are

---

[88] Tirmīdhī: 1924; Abu Dāwūd: 4941.
[89] Bukhārī: 7422, 7453; Muslim: 2751 b; Ibn Mājah: 194.

few and far between, which shows that Allāh's 🕮 mercy is prevalent over His anger. In one place, Allāh 🕮 says:

$$وَرَحْمَتِي وَسِعَتْ كُلَّ شَيْءٍ ۚ$$

And My mercy extends to everything. [90]

He also says:

$$كَتَبَ عَلَىٰ نَفْسِهِ الرَّحْمَةَ ۚ$$

He has fixed Mercy upon Himself. [91]

Allāh 🕮 loves showing mercy and deals with us with mercy. As we are reading now, our breathing is comfortable; we are living with āfiyat [peace of mind and body]. This is all a mercy from Allāh 🕮. It is Allāh's 🕮 mercy which allows us to walk, talk, to worship him, and to give charity. His mercy is constantly with us. Only sometimes, Allāh 🕮 becomes displeased with His servant, because of his misdeeds, and, therefore, gives him a taste of His displeasure, but His mercy always overpowers His anger.

100 Parts of Mercy

It is mentioned in a Hadīth that Allāh 🕮 has divided His mercy into one hundred parts. Of these, He has distributed only one part to the entire creation and has distributed this one part between them. Just one part of mercy for all humanity, jinn and animals. This also includes predatory, wild animals, who have also received some of this portion of mercy. The manifestation of this mercy in a wild animal is the love it has for its offspring. It feeds it, nurses it, cares for it, hunts for it and protects it. The human's share in this one portion of mercy can be seen in the way he deals with his friends, family and his love

---

[90] Qur'ān 7:156.
[91] Qur'ān 6:12.

for his children. The other ninety nine portions of mercy are kept by Allāh ﷻ.[92]

At the time of reckoning, in the hereafter, when Allāh ﷻ will be greatly displeased with man, he shall take to task the wretched, wicked, and evil people of the world, who were tyrants and oppressors and will throw them into the hellfire. Then the reckoning for the rest of the human beings will start. Allāh ﷻ will then not only use these ninety-nine remaining portions of mercy, but will also use the one portion He distributed amongst the creation, so a total of one hundred portions of mercy will come into manifestation at the time of reckoning.

SUFYĀN THAWRĪ'S STATEMENT

This is why Sufyān Thawrī ﵀ used to say, 'I would <u>not</u> like my own father to take my reckoning, because – ربي خيرلي من ابي – my Rabb is better for me than my father.' Even my father would not show as much mercy to me as my Rabb. So when Allāh ﷻ will start taking account of man, He will show an enormous amount of mercy.[93]

In his *Munājāt*, Hājī Imdādullāh Muhājir Makkī ﵀ used to supplicate in the following way:

رہے گانہ کچھ نقد عصیاں سے میرا، لگے گا جو رحمت کا بازار تیرا

When the gates of Your Mercy open on the Day of Reckoning,
I have hope that none of my sins shall remain.

SINS TURNED INTO VIRTUES

Allāh ﷻ will show so much mercy that even the sins of some fortunate people will be converted to virtues, for which they will then be rewarded. Allāh ﷻ will summon a certain servant and curtain him. He will then ask the servant about

---

[92] Bukhārī: 6469; Muslim: 2752 b, 2752 c, 2753 c; Ibn Mājah: 4434.
[93] Majmū'atur-Rasāil Ibn Abi Dunyā: 37.

a range of sins he had committed, and the servant will confess to everything he had done. Then Allāh ﷻ will reply: "I concealed your sins from the people in the world, today I will forgive you". Furthermore, Allāh ﷻ will then command for his sins to be converted to good deeds. The servant will say in reply to this favour of Allāh ﷻ: "O Allāh, there are still some sins which I am unaccounted for!" It is mentioned in the Hadīth that Allāh ﷻ will smile with the reaction of the servant and his greed for the favours of Allāh ﷻ and will even change the sins which were unaccounted for! [Smiling could mean becoming happy and rewarding].

ALLAH IS MORE MERCIFUL THAN A MOTHER

Once Rasūlullāh ﷺ was returning from an expedition, and amongst the prisoners of war, was a woman who was looking for her missing baby. This child was unaccounted for amidst the chaos of war. The woman was frantically searching for her child, but the search was unsuccessful. Every child she would see, she would hold close to her chest and portray love, then return the child to its mother. Rasūlullāh ﷺ was observing this scene and said to the Sahāba ﷺ, 'If she was to find her child, do you think that she would throw it in a fire?' The Sahāba replied, 'No, as long as she is able to do so.' Rasūlullāh ﷺ said:

$$\text{الله ارحم بعباده من هذه بولدها}$$

Allāh is more merciful with His bondsmen than this mother with her child. [94]

On another occasion, Rasūlullāh ﷺ was with the Sahāba when a woman approached him with a child in her arms. She asked: "Ya Rasūlallāh! ﷺ, Is Allāh not more merciful to His slaves than a mother to her children?" The Prophet ﷺ replied in the affirmative. She then posed an amazing question:

---

[94] Bukhārī: 5999, Muslim: 2574.

"So no mother would throw her child in a fire?" Rasūlullāh 🕮 burst into tears. Then he raised his head and said:

ان الله لا يدخل من عباده النار الا المارد المتمرد

الذي يتمرد على الله وأبى أن يقول لا اله الا الله

"Allāh will throw nobody in the fire, except the rebellious, disobedient, mutinous, who rebelled against Allāh and refused to utter 'Laa ilaahā illallāh ...'"
95

The fire has only been made for individuals like this. It has not been made for those who accept the authority of the Almighty.

THE HELL FIRE IS NOT FOR THE OBEDIENT ONES

My beloved honourable teacher Shaykhul Hadīth Maulānā Islāmulhaq Sahib 🕮 used to say, 'Jahannam is not made for the believers. It is made for the stubborn types, those who refuse to accept Allāh's lordship and bear hatred towards Allāh.' If a Mu'min does enter the fire due to excessive sinning and disobedience, it will not be as a punishment, but to cleanse them of their sins, similar to how rust is removed from metals using heat. The metal is then knocked with a hammer to strengthen it. If this process is not undertaken, the metal would eventually weaken and erode. Hadhrat Shaykhul Hadīth Sahib would also mention the example of a believer in the fire is like a child who goes to play football in the rain, as a result of which his clothes are covered with mud. When he reaches home, his mother will stop him at the entrance of the home and will not allow him to step into the house in this dirty state. She will ensure he removes his boots and may even reprimand him for not looking after himself in the rain. She will pick him up, avoiding the carpet and seat him directly in the bathroom. She will bathe him and continue to reprimand him

---

95 Ibn Mājah, Mishkāt, Misbāh uz Zujajah: Vol 4, Pg.258.

as she is bathing him. This is the example of a believer who lived in the disobedience of Allāh ﷻ. Allāh ﷻ will cleanse him in the fire from his sins and reprimand him for his lack of obedience and discipline. When he is cleansed, he will be removed and instructed to bathe in a river outside Jannah. He will jump into the river and all effects of burning will disappear. He will have fresh skin, then he will be admitted in to Jannah.

The final person to be removed from Jahannam will be asked by Allāh ﷻ about what he now wants. He will pose his demands to Allāh ﷻ and tire himself with his demands. Allāh ﷻ will ask if he has any more requests. He will say no, then Allāh ﷻ will grant him everything he asked for, and will give him a Jannah ten times the size of this world. This will be the size of the smallest Jannah. Imagine how the greatest Jannah will be. This is a manifestation of the mercy of Allāh ﷻ. Allāh ﷻ does not wish to punish anybody. Allāh ﷻ says in the Qur'ān, in the last ayat of the fifth Juz:

$$\text{مَّا يَفْعَلُ اللَّهُ بِعَذَابِكُم إِن شَكَرْتُمْ وَآمَنتُمْ ۚ وَكَانَ اللَّهُ شَاكِرًا عَلِيمًا ۞}$$

What will Allāh do with punishing you, if you are grateful
and have faith?' Allāh Himself is appreciative and the All-Knowing. [96]

ALLĀH IS EASY TO PLEASE

Allāh ﷻ gets happy with one sajdāh, with one Subhānallāh, one Alhamdulillāh. Allāh ﷻ is very kind, very giving and very generous and it is very easy for us to please Him. We do not need to engage in long, strenuous acts of worship to please Him. If a slave exerts a small amount of effort, Allāh ﷻ will be pleased with him, to the extent that Rasūlullāh ﷺ said:

ان الله ليرضى عن العبد ان يأكل الأكلة

فيحمده عليها ويشرب الشربة فيحمده عليها

---

[96] Qur'ān 4:147.

"When a person after eating one morsel says 'Alhamdulillāh' [from the depth of his heart], Allāh ﷻ gets pleased with him. Similar is the case with drinking a chilled drink and praising Allāh."

We have been instructed to read at Iftaar:

ذهب الظمأ وابتلت العروق وثبت الأجر ان شاء الله

"The thirst has been quenched, the pores/veins have been satiated and the reward has been established Inshā-Allāh." [97]

SŪRAH FĀTIHA DIVIDED BETWEEN THE RABB AND HIS SLAVE

In the Hadīth of Abu Hurairah ﷺ, Rasūlullāh ﷺ said that Allāh ﷻ said, "I have divided Sūrah Fātiha into two parts, one is for my servant and the other is for Me:

When the servant says: الْحَمْدُ لِلَّهِ رَبِّ الْعَالَمِينَ
Allāh says, "My servant has praised Me."

When the servant says: الرَّحْمَنِ الرَّحِيمِ
Allāh says, "My servant has honoured me highly."

When the servant says: مَالِكِ يَوْمِ الدِّينِ
Allāh says, "My servant has exalted me."

When the servant says: إِيَّاكَ نَعْبُدُ وَإِيَّاكَ نَسْتَعِينُ
Allāh says, "This is between Me and My servant, and My servant shall have what he asks for."

When the servant says:

---

[97] Abu Dāwūd.

اهْدِنَا الصِّرَاطَ الْمُسْتَقِيمَ صِرَاطَ الَّذِينَ أَنْعَمْتَ عَلَيْهِمْ غَيْرِ الْمَغْضُوبِ عَلَيْهِمْ وَلَا الضَّالِّينَ

Allāh says, "This is for My servant, and My servant shall have what he has asked for." [98]

This is why we should continuously recite Sūrah Fātiha and why we are instructed to make it a part of every unit of salāh. We should recite it with full concentration and full conviction that Allāh ﷻ is listening to everything we say and is responding fittingly. Allāh ﷻ will give us whatever we ask for. Allāh ﷻ is the Most Merciful and to please Him is very easy, which is why Allāh ﷻ uses the words Ar-Raḥmān and Ar-Rahīm to describe Himself.

THE PROPHETS RECEIVED THE GREATEST SHARE OF MERCY

Allāh ﷻ is merciful, and Allāh ﷻ has distributed mercy amongst His creation. Some of His creation have received greater portions, others have received less. The Messengers ﷺ were given the greatest amounts of mercy. Amongst the Messengers, the one who received the greatest share was the leader of both worlds, Muhammad ﷺ. He was so kind and merciful that Allāh ﷻ declared in the Qur'ān:

وَمَا أَرْسَلْنَاكَ إِلَّا رَحْمَةً لِّلْعَالَمِينَ ۞

O' Nabi, we have sent you as a mercy for the whole universe. [99]

Allāh ﷻ says in Sūrah Taubah:

قُلْ أُذُنُ خَيْرٍ لَّكُمْ يُؤْمِنُ بِاللَّهِ وَيُؤْمِنُ لِلْمُؤْمِنِينَ وَرَحْمَةٌ لِّلَّذِينَ آمَنُوا مِنكُمْ ۚ وَالَّذِينَ يُؤْذُونَ رَسُولَ اللَّهِ لَهُمْ عَذَابٌ أَلِيمٌ ۞

---

[98] Muslim.
[99] Qur'ān 21:107.

Tell them, 'He is all ears of good for you.' He believes in Allāh, believes in the
Mu'mineen and is a <u>mercy</u> to those of you who have Īmān. There is a painful
punishment for those who harass the Rasūl of Allāh. [100]

Allāh ﷻ also mentions at the end of Sūrah Taubah:

$$لَقَدْ جَاءَكُمْ رَسُولٌ مِّنْ أَنفُسِكُمْ عَزِيزٌ عَلَيْهِ مَا عَنِتُّمْ$$

$$حَرِيصٌ عَلَيْكُم بِالْمُؤْمِنِينَ رَءُوفٌ رَّحِيمٌ ۞$$

"Undoubtedly a Rasūl from yourselves has come to you. The difficulties that
afflict you are very distressing to him. He is anxious for you and extremely
<u>*forgiving*</u> *and* <u>*merciful*</u> *towards the Mu'mineen."* [101]

The Messenger ﷺ says himself in a Hadīth:

$$إِنَّمَا أَنَا رَحْمَةٌ مُهْدَاةٌ$$

"I am but a <u>mercy</u> and a source of guidance." [102]

THE SOFT NATURE OF RAHMATUL-LIL-ĀLAMEEN ﷺ

This is why the Messenger ﷺ was very soft spoken and very soft-hearted.
From amongst his greatest characteristics were his gentleness, his
compassion, and soft nature. These characteristics were not exclusive to the
time after receiving Prophet-hood, but were inherent from before. He was so
kind, gentle, and considerate that the people of Makkāh would respect him and
love him for these characteristics. He was referred to as a noble person, and
this nobility had already begun to manifest from his childhood.

---

[100] Qur'ān 9:61.

[101] Qur'ān 9:128.

[102] Mishkāt.

The Messenger ﷺ was brought up as an orphan. His father passed away whilst he was in his mother's womb, and his mother passed away by the time he was six. His grandfather Abdul Muttalib also died when he was only eight. He was brought up in the home of his uncle Abu Tālib. Abu Tālib had other children too and was not considered a wealthy man. When food was prepared for the children, it was placed in a tray from which they would all eat. Muhammad ﷺ would abstain from rushing to the tray. He would wait for others to finish and then eat whatever was left over. This young child was not afraid of hunger but was very careful not to be greedy for food. It stayed like this for a while until Abu Tālib noticed what was going on, that his children were taking the food for themselves and Muhammad ﷺ was only having the leftovers and, at times, was even going hungry. Due to this situation, he ordered that Muhammad's ﷺ meals should be served separately so he could eat properly. He knew if he continued serving food in the same way, this child would never complain and would rather go hungry due to his nobility and kindness to the other children.

Many days passed like this in his orphan youth. These experiences only made his heart stronger and more accepting. When Allāh ﷻ created the souls and checked them to see the best, he saw it was the soul of the final Messenger ﷺ. He blessed this soul with the nūr of Prophethood, then chose the other messengers and allocated a part of this nūr to each of them. This is how Muhammad ﷺ, was sent as a mercy for all types of creation; humans, jinns, the angels, the creatures of air, land and sea, and even the archangel Jibra'īl عليه السلام.[103]

MERCY FOR THE MALĀ'IKAH

On one occasion, the Messenger ﷺ asked Jibra'īl if he had benefitted from the mercy of Rasūlullāh ﷺ, so Jibra'īl replied: "Yes! Before your Prophethood, I was forever afraid that Allāh ﷻ could get displeased with me. But Allāh ﷻ sent

---

[103] Ash-Shifa.

you and chose me to deliver the message to you, and Allāh 🕮 praised me in the same Qur'ān I was entrusted to deliver to you. Allāh 🕮 said:

$$\text{عَلَّمَهُ شَدِيدُ الْقُوَىٰ ۞ ذُو مِرَّةٍ فَاسْتَوَىٰ ۞ وَهُوَ بِالْأُفُقِ الْأَعْلَىٰ ۞}$$

He has been taught by one who is of tremendous might and who is extremely powerful. He appeared in his original form when he was on the highest part of the horizon. [104]

And:

$$\text{إِنَّهُ لَقَوْلُ رَسُولٍ كَرِيمٍ ۞ ذِي قُوَّةٍ عِندَ ذِي الْعَرْشِ مَكِينٍ ۞ مُّطَاعٍ ثَمَّ أَمِينٍ ۞}$$

Undoubtedly this is a word brought by an honoured messenger who is powerful and of high rank in the sight of the Owner of the Throne. He is also obeyed and trustworthy. [105]

Jibra'īl 🕮 meant to say that these verses put my heart at ease. So now I don't fear a wretched ending.

MERCY FOR THE JINN'S

How was the Prophet 🕮 a source of mercy for the jinn's? He met with the jinns seven times. A large number of jinns came to meet him, thus the Messenger 🕮 invited them to Islam, which they duly accepted. They posed a few questions to him which he answered. Jinns would frequent the Masjid of the Messenger 🕮 and would pray salāh behind him. They would also sit and listen whilst he delivered his talks. Even within the jinn community, they have great scholars of Hadīth who have heard from the Messenger himself and pass on the knowledge to their communities. Some jinns even visit institutes like

---

[104] Qur'ān 53:5-7.
[105] Qur'ān 81:19-21.

Darul Uloom Deoband in order to benefit from the lessons of Hadīth. They enjoy the environment of the Masjid also and pass their time within the Masjid.

MERCY FOR THE ANIMALS

Rasūlullāh ﷺ was also a mercy for all types of animals. He taught us the rights of animals hundreds of years before Western animal rights organizations were established. He taught us the rights that animals have over us more than 1400 years ago. He ﷺ said:

في كل ذات كبد رطبة أجر

"There is reward to be earnt in every being which possesses a liver [which requires water to survive]."

He told us about the story of the prostitute who spent her life in sin, but gave a thirsty dog water to drink, so Allāh ﷻ forgave her. [106] If we have pets, then we should look after them like they deserve to be treated. The Messenger ﷺ mentioned the story of a woman who worshipped Allāh ﷻ a lot, but would keep her cat tied up and would not look after it. She would not even let the cat loose to eat the insects of the ground. Allāh ﷻ overlooked all her good deeds and punished her because of her treatment of this cat. [107] The Messenger ﷺ passed by a camel which was making strange sounds. Nabi ﷺ approached it and heard its complaints. He called the owner of the camel and told him of the complaint that 'you don't feed it enough and you burden it with great loads'. He instructed the man to fear Allāh ﷻ with regards to these animals. He explained that although the camel was dumb and unable to articulate its feelings, this did not mean it could be abused or treated unfairly. [108] Animals must be fed well, looked after well and kept healthy.

---

[106] Bukhārī.

[107] Bukhārī, Muslim.

[108] Ash-Shifa.

HIS ﷺ KINDNESS TO HIS COMPANIONS

He was a rahmah and a mercy for all. His soft nature and generosity were well-known. This was due to his compassion and mercy. He would supplicate on behalf of the companions. Whilst sending Muaadh bin. Jabal ؓ to Yemen, he prayed for him:

حفظك الله من بين يديك ومن خلفك وعن يمينك

وعن شمالك ودرا عنك شرور الأنس والجن

May Allāh safeguard and protect you from the front and the back, from your left and from your right, and repel from you the evils of Jinn and Ins [humans].

HIS ﷺ SPEECH PRIOR TO HIS DEATH

A few days before his death he stood on the pulpit addressing the companions, praying for them: "May Allāh bless you and do good for you, may He accept your good deeds, may He enable you to do more good and have mercy on you..." and the duā went on. His soft nature was such that neither did he cause anybody harm nor could he bear to see any sort of maltreatment of others. Nor could he listen to any statement which would hurt the feelings of a fellow human being, to the extent that if he was told about the ill-comment of another person, he would ask not to be told the details just because he didn't want any negative feelings to enter his heart against that person. He would ensure his heart was always clean.

On one occasion, the Messenger ﷺ was making his way to Khaybar on camel back, and to the side of him was one companion, whose stead was slightly faster. His foot hit the leg of the Messenger ﷺ, which caused him great discomfort. He had a whip, with which he reprimanded this companion, that there was no need to rush and you could have been more careful. The companion apologised and distanced his camel from the camel of Rasūlullāh

75

. The following day, the Messenger ﷺ sent for him to be brought. He was scared of what the Messenger ﷺ might say to him following the previous day's incident. When he arrived, the Messenger ﷺ apologised for his reaction and asked for his forgiveness. He then offered eighty [80] camels as a compensation to the companion for just one scolding! His heart was so soft it was unable to bear even this much of a reaction. This was his gentle nature, which extended to all of Allāh's ﷻ creation.

Hadhrat Anas ؓ was only ten when he came to stay in his service. He stayed in the company of the Messenger ﷺ, until he was twenty. He says, 'during these ten years, never once did the Prophet ﷺ say 'uf' to me, nor did he question why I had done something, nor why I had not done something.' [109] At times, even those with the gentlest dispositions are moved to anger, but the Prophet ﷺ would not even say 'uf', let alone become angry or lash out. The Messenger ﷺ was sent as a mercy for all, and through his blessings, rahmah has also been transferred into his Ummah. In all situations, the Muslim Ummah should portray this quality of rahmah and, in particular, those who are close to Allāh ﷻ, should treat others with extreme kindness.

THE KINDNESS OF KHAWAJĀ MU'ĪNUDDĪN CHISTĪ AJMERĪ ؒ

An enemy of Hadhrat Khawajā Chishtī Mu'īnuddīn Ajmerī ؒ bribed an assassin to kill Hadhrat Khawajā Sāhib. The man came to a gathering of Hadhrat Khawajā Sāhib, hiding a dagger, with the intention to kill him. He sat close to him and was still musing about how best to execute his plan. Suddenly, Khawajā Sāhib quietly said to him, 'Complete the task for which you have come.' The man began to sweat and pleaded for forgiveness. He placed the dagger in front of Hadhrat and requested Khawajā Sāhib to kill him in retaliation. Hadhrat Khawajā Sāhib refused, saying, 'We are the people of Allāh. We make duā for even those who cause us difficulties, and you have not

---

[109] Mishkāt.

harmed me in any way, so why should I harm you? Put the dagger away before anyone sees it.' When the gathering finished, Hadhrat Khawajā Sāhib called for some money and gifts and offered it to him. The man was deeply affected by this and became a mureed and an aashiq of Hadhrat Khawajā Sāhib.

THE INCIDENT OF HADHRAT CHIRĀG DEHLAWĪ ﷜

Hadhrat Shaykh Naseerudeen Chirāg Dehlawī ﷜ was once busy in Murāqabā [contemplation]. A *Qalandar* secretly entered his place of worship and began to stab him with a knife. His blood began to flow outside. Hadhrat Shaykh ﷜ didn't cause any commotion though he was being attacked. People were perturbed by the sight of blood flowing from his chamber. When they went inside and saw the *Qalandar* with the knife, they became very angry and fell on him from all sides. Hadhrat Shaykh ﷜ was bandaged up. He stopped the people from becoming angry and called for some money saying, 'This will be a compensation for any difficulty you may have faced whilst stabbing me.' These are examples of the soft and merciful nature of those who are close to Allāh ﷾.

The Prophet ﷺ said to his Sahābā:

$$أرحم أمتي بأمتي ابوبكر$$

'The most merciful from amongst my Ummah to my Ummah is Abubakr'. [110]

It is because of the barakah of the Prophet ﷺ that Hadhrat Abubakr ﷺ epitomised this quality. Likewise, the rahmah that the Ummah possess is a reflection of the Prophet's qualities.

UMMAH OF MERCY

The difficulties that the Muslim Ummah faces at the hands of other communities is undeniable. The Danish cartoons and various social media

---

[110] Tirmīdhī, Mishkāt.

campaigns are examples of this, yet the Ummah exercises patience and abstains from knee jerk reactions. We say, 'your actions are with you and our actions are with us'. This is not freedom of speech. It is freedom to insult; it is freedom of abuse. If this freedom of abuse is allowed to continue, this society will crumble and this country will be destroyed. Lawlessness and disorder are rife in this country. There is a lack of respect for elders, and of mercy towards youngsters. Respect for parents and teachers has sadly disappeared. The main reason for arguments, dishonesty and disloyalty, is this concept of 'freedom of speech' which is so widespread. If this is controlled and rules are put in place for children to respect their parents and teachers, society will resume some order.

Shaykh Yūnus Dāmat Barakātuhum, on one occasion, made a duā asking for the protection of this country. We too should make duā for the guidance of the people, that Allāh ﷻ creates rahmah in their hearts, and that Allāh ﷻ guides them to mend their ways. We are not terrorists and we do not want anything bad to happen to this country.

We should also pray for protection against treachery and scheming. Our Prophet ﷺ has given us instruction. He said, 'Allāh ﷻ says: 'O My slaves! I have made injustice harām upon myself and I have prohibited it among you too, so do not do oppress one another'. [111] Islam is categorically against terrorism. Islam preaches only love and respect. Islam has invited people towards it through rahmah, not through the force of the sword. Political advancement and religious advancement are two distinct things, and, although Islam may have advanced politically by means of the sword, religiously it has advanced because of its teachings. People were able to see what Islam had to offer, they studied its teachings and the Qur'ān. They observed the lives of the Sahāba. The exemplary characteristics of the Sahāba had such a profound effect on them that they began to flock towards Islam. One Sahābī ﷺ would travel to an area and the entire region would accept Islam

---

[111] Muslim.

at his hands. A hāfiz would travel to remote places and people would flock towards him to embrace Islam. There are examples in history of Huffāz, Ulamā, and friends of Allāh ﷻ visiting places like China, Indonesia and the islands of Maldives and Malta and other countries where there was no sign of Islam. However their Islamic code of conduct and character led the locals to accept this faith. Islam was spread by peace, by manners and by good morals. Islam and terrorism have no link.

We have always been taught that Allāh ﷻ is the Most Merciful, that He is Ar-Rahmān and Ar-Rahīm. We have been taught that the Prophet ﷺ is a mercy for mankind and that because of him, his Ummah also possesses this quality. As Muslims, we approach with mercy and we dislike causing any sort of difficulty to anyone. This is the very essence of our religion and this is why we recite bismillāh repeatedly. In Sūrah Fātiha and Sūrah Rahmān, these qualities of Allāh ﷻ are displayed. The Messenger ﷺ has said, 'Be merciful to those who dwell on the earth and the one in the heaven will have mercy on you.' We must refrain from all types of abuse, whether it's physical abuse, mental abuse, emotional abuse, psychological abuse or any other type of abuse. These are the beautiful teachings of Islam.

May Allāh ﷻ create this rahmah within us and protect us from harming anyone. We should aim to create tenderness and compassion within ourselves. We should read about the kindness, softness and gentleness of the Messenger ﷺ and adopt these qualities within us. Make an effort to read *al-Shamaail al-Muhammadiyyah*, written by Īmām Tirmīdhī ﷫, and its commentary *Khasaail-e-Nabawi*, written by Hadhrat Shaykhul Hadīth Maulānā Muhammad Zakarīyyā Kāndhalwī ﷫. We pray that Allāh ﷻ endows us with these qualities so that we become beacons of compassion and tenderness. Āmīn!

AN AMAZING DUĀ FOR DEBT

Previously, we delved into the exegesis of 'Rahmān' and 'Rahīm', regarding which another hadīth comes to mind wherein the Prophet ﷺ mentioned these two attributes of Allāh ﷻ. Once a sahābī ؓ requested the Prophet ﷺ to make duā for him as he had a lot of debt. He was told to pray with certain words to remove the burden of debt upon him and gain the help of Allāh ﷻ in freeing him from it. [112] In a narration of Ibn Abī Shaybah ؓ, 'Abdullāh ibn Thābit ؓ says: The Messenger of Allāh ﷺ would himself recite these words and give them great importance: [113]

اللّٰهُمَّ فَارِجَ الهَمِّ وَكَاشِفَ الغَمِّ مُجِيْبَ دَعْوَةِ
المُضْطَرِّين، رَحْمٰنَ الدنيا وَالآخِرَةِوَرَحيمَهُما، اِرْحَمْنِي اليَومَ رَحْمَةً
وَاسِعَةً تُغْنِيْنِيْ بِها عَنْ رَحْمَةٍ مَنْ سِواكَ

'O Allāh, O remover of suffering, reliever from agony, responder to the prayers of the distressed, and All-beneficent and All-merciful in this world and the next. Have mercy upon me this day, such bountiful mercy which frees me from having the need of mercy of any other than You.'

What a wonderful duā our Prophet ﷺ has taught us, wherein we acknowledge that only Allāh ﷻ can remove agonies, anxieties and distress. Only Allāh ﷻ listens to the prayers of the heartbroken and helpless. Allāh ﷻ is the beneficent Rabb of this world and the hereafter. So when only You, O Allāh! ﷻ, are the all-merciful, we ask only You to bless us and bestow upon us such wonderful blessings that through them we may become detached from the love of this world. We may become free, become independent. We are not in need of anybody but You.

Our Prophet ﷺ taught his companion ؓ to pray this duā that Allāh ﷻ may dissolve his debt. Hence the companion ؓ prayed and Allāh ﷻ removed his debt. If anyone is under the strain of debt, they should learn this duā as it shall greatly benefit them Inshā-Allāh.

---

[112] Al-Durral-Manthūr: 1/24.
[113] Musnaf Ibn Abī Shaybah: 6/109.

ANOTHER DUĀ FOR PAYING OFF DEBTS

In another Hadīth, 'Ali ﷺ narrates:

A slave who had made a contract with his master to pay for his freedom, came to me and said: 'I am unable to fulfil my obligation, so help me.' I said to him: 'Shall I not teach you a supplication which the Messenger of Allāh ﷺ taught me? It will surely prove so effective that if you have a debt as large as a huge mountain, Allāh ﷺ will surely pay it for you. He said: "Say:

اللَّهُمَّ اكْفِنِي بِحَلَالِكَ عَنْ حَرَامِكَ وَأَغْنِنِي بِفَضْلِكَ عَمَّنْ سِوَاكَ

O Allāh! Grant me enough of what You make lawful so that I may dispense with what You make unlawful, and enable me by Your Grace to dispense with all but You.'" [114]

In this day and age, our thoughts and desires constantly incline us towards the unlawful, harām. We have become avaricious and greedy, yearning to gain wealth and riches at any cost. The faster the better. Many buy lottery tickets in the hope of hitting the jackpot. May Allāh ﷺ protect us.

Some are caught up in the drug trade. Discretely and cautiously they smuggle drugs into the country and sell them on. They are not caught. A profit is made. And now the greed sets in. They become smugglers and dealers, causing people to commit sin, intoxicating people, destroying people's lives. Every penny they make is unlawful, harām money. Sin upon sin.

May Allāh ﷺ save us from inclination towards the harām. We should not even contemplate VAT scams, false insurance claims, and other unlawful paths. 'O Allāh, grant us sufficient lawful sustenance so that our thoughts and inclinations never stray towards unlawful sustenance.' We will receive our sustenance, no matter what. Our responsibility is that we earn it in a lawful manner and save ourselves from unlawful manner.

---

[114]Jami' at-Tirmīdhī: 3563.

Muftī Zaynul Ābidīn, a saint of *Tablīghī Jamā'at* from Pakistan, says that the example of sustenance is that of a big room. The room is full of your sustenance [that you will receive during your lifetime], which is fixed. It is written from Allāh 🌸 that this sustenance will reach this person. Sustenance is fixed, it is in the room. However, there are two entrances to the room. One entrance is halāl [lawful] and the other entrance to the room is harām [unlawful]. It is your responsibility to open the doors and go inside. Whether you enter from the halāl door or harām door, you will receive the same sustenance. No more and no less. However, if you enter from the halāl door you will not be held to account, but if you enter from the harām door, you will be have to suffer grave consequences. You are destined to receive your sustenance regardless, yet from which door you obtain it, is your responsibility. So be careful about which door you enter from and from where your sustenance comes.

There is an event from the life of Sayyidunā Ali 🌸 that relates to this point. 'Once Sayyidunā Ali bin Abi Tālib 🌸 passed by a Masjid. He wanted to pray a few rak'āts of salāh in the Masjid. He saw a man standing at the door of the Masjid, who offered to hold his horse for him so he could go inside and pray. Sayyidunā Ali 🌸 thanked him, went inside and prayed. He took out two dirhams [money] from his pocket intending to give it to the man, in return for his kindness. However, he found that the horse was still there, but without its reins. The man had run off with the reins. He gave the two dirhams to another person to purchase a reign for his horse. At the marketplace, the man found the exact reins that the thief had stolen, who preceded to sell them to him for two dirhams. He returned with the reins. Sayyidunā Ali 🌸 said with tears in his eyes, 'Indeed, that person prevented himself from lawful sustenance by stealing the reins. Had he remained here, he would have received the same two dirham's but in a halāl way with my duās. But now he has received them in a harām way.' [115]

---

[115] Mujāhid, Abdul-Malik, Gems and Jewels, London: Darussalam, 2004, p.63.

May Allāh ﷻ give us the tawfeeq to utilize halāl means for earning our livelihood. May Allāh ﷻ protect us from harām. Āmīn.

VERSE 3

مَالِكِ يَوْمِ الدِّينِ ﴿٣﴾

[The] Master of the Day of Requital.

There are two ways in which this verse can be recited: Mālik [مَالِكِ], stretching the first vowel; or Malik [مَلِكِ], without stretching it. The word 'Malik' means king, as in 'King of the Day of Requital', because kingship on that day will belong to Allāh ﷻ, and Allāh ﷻ alone. Recitation with 'Malik' takes the following verses into consideration:

يَوْمَ هُم بَارِزُونَ ۖ لَا يَخْفَىٰ عَلَى اللَّهِ مِنْهُمْ شَيْءٌ ۚ

لِّمَنِ الْمُلْكُ الْيَوْمَ ۖ لِلَّهِ الْوَاحِدِ الْقَهَّارِ ﴾

The day they will come in open view. Nothing about them will remain hidden from Allāh. [He will ask and then answer]. To whom belongs the kingdom today? To Allāh alone, the One, the All-Dominant. [116]

The recitation with 'Mālik', i.e. the stretched vowel, takes the following verses into consideration:

كَلَّا بَلْ تُكَذِّبُونَ بِالدِّينِ ﴾ وَإِنَّ عَلَيْكُمْ لَحَافِظِينَ ﴾ كِرَامًا كَاتِبِينَ ﴾

يَعْلَمُونَ مَا تَفْعَلُونَ ﴾ إِنَّ الْأَبْرَارَ لَفِي نَعِيمٍ ﴾ وَإِنَّ الْفُجَّارَ لَفِي جَحِيمٍ ﴾

يَصْلَوْنَهَا يَوْمَ الدِّينِ ﴾ وَمَا هُمْ عَنْهَا بِغَائِبِينَ ﴾ وَمَا أَدْرَاكَ مَا يَوْمُ الدِّينِ ﴾

ثُمَّ مَا أَدْرَاكَ مَا يَوْمُ الدِّينِ ﴾ يَوْمَ لَا تَمْلِكُ نَفْسٌ لِّنَفْسٍ شَيْئًا ۖ وَالْأَمْرُ يَوْمَئِذٍ لِّلَّهِ ﴾

---

[116] Qur'ān 40:16.

Never! [One should never be heedless towards him.] But you deny the Requital, while [appointed] over you there are watchers, who are noble, writers [of the deeds], who know whatever you do. Surely the righteous will be in bliss, and the sinners in Hell, in which they will enter on the Day of Requital, and they will not [be able to] keep away from it. And what may let you know what the Day of Requital is? Again, what may let you know what the Day of Requital is? A Day when no one will have the ownership of anything for anyone! And command, on that Day, will belong to Allāh [alone]. [117]

And:

يَوْمَ نَحْشُرُ الْمُتَّقِينَ إِلَى الرَّحْمَٰنِ وَفْدًا ۝ وَنَسُوقُ الْمُجْرِمِينَ إِلَىٰ جَهَنَّمَ وِرْدًا ۝

لَّا يَمْلِكُونَ الشَّفَاعَةَ إِلَّا مَنِ اتَّخَذَ عِندَ الرَّحْمَٰنِ عَهْدًا ۝

The day We will assemble the God-fearing before the All-Merciful [Allāh] as guests, and will drive the sinners towards the Jahannam as herds of cattle [are driven] towards water, none will have power to intercede, except the one who has entered into a covenant with the All-Merciful [Allāh]. [118]

The word, 'Mālik', denotes mastery and power. On the Day of Requital, Allāh ﷻ alone will possess all power and mastery over everything. People will avail nothing for each other, as Allāh ﷻ states:

فَإِذَا جَاءَتِ الصَّاخَّةُ ۝ يَوْمَ يَفِرُّ الْمَرْءُ مِنْ أَخِيهِ ۝ وَأُمِّهِ وَأَبِيهِ ۝

وَصَاحِبَتِهِ وَبَنِيهِ ۝ لِكُلِّ امْرِئٍ مِّنْهُمْ يَوْمَئِذٍ شَأْنٌ يُغْنِيهِ ۝

So when the Deafening Noise will occur, the Day when one will flee from his brother, and from his mother and father, and from his wife and sons, every one of them will be too engaged in his own affairs to care for others. [119]

---

[117] Qur'ān 82:9-19.

[118] Qur'ān 19:85-87.

[119] Qur'ān 80:33-37.

This is what is meant by 'none will have power to intercede' and 'command, on that Day, will belong to Allāh'. Allāh ﷻ is both, Mālik and Malik – as well as Mālik-al-Mulūk and Malik-al-Mulūk: Master and King; Master of all Masters and King of all Kings.

HADĪTH QUDSĪ

Abu Dardā ﷺ relates a hadīth, stating that:

> Allāh's Messenger ﷺ said that Allāh says, 'Indeed, I am Allāh. There is no god but me. I am the owner of Kings and the King of Kings. The hearts of kings are in my hand. When my slaves obey me, I make the hearts of their kings full of compassion and mercy; and when my slaves disobey me, I make the hearts of their kings full of wrath and vengeance, and they punish them most severely. So don't busy yourselves with praying against kings, and [instead] busy yourselves with supplication and pleading to me and I will suffice for you.' [120]

Keeping this hadīth in mind, we should invoke Allāh ﷻ to guide our leaders and soften their hearts, rather than curse them or wish ill upon them.

Allāh ﷻ also mentions the quality of being Mālik-al-mulk in the following verse:

قُلِ اللَّهُمَّ مَالِكَ الْمُلْكِ تُؤْتِي الْمُلْكَ مَن تَشَاءُ وَتَنزِعُ الْمُلْكَ مِمَّن تَشَاءُ وَتُعِزُّ مَن تَشَاءُ وَتُذِلُّ مَن تَشَاءُ ۖ بِيَدِكَ الْخَيْرُ ۖ إِنَّكَ عَلَىٰ كُلِّ شَيْءٍ قَدِيرٌ ۞ تُولِجُ اللَّيْلَ فِي النَّهَارِ وَتُولِجُ النَّهَارَ فِي اللَّيْلِ ۖ وَتُخْرِجُ الْحَيَّ مِنَ الْمَيِّتِ وَتُخْرِجُ الْمَيِّتَ مِنَ الْحَيِّ ۖ وَتَرْزُقُ مَن تَشَاءُ بِغَيْرِ حِسَابٍ ۞

---

[120] Al Mu'jam al-Awsat of Tabrānī, Mishkāt.

Say: "O Allāh, O Owner of the Kingdom, You give kingdom to whom You will, and take kingdom away from whom You will; and You bestow honour on whom You will, and bring disgrace to whom You will. In your hand lies the betterment [of everyone]. You are surely powerful over everything. You make the night enter into the day, and make the day enter into the night; and You bring the living out from the dead, and You bring the dead out from the living, and You give beyond measure to whom You will."

121

VIRTUES OF THE VERSE 'MĀLIKUL MULK'

Regarding the virtues of these verses, Mufti Muhammad Shafī ﷴ relates a hadīth from *Rūh-al-Ma'āni* with reference to dailamī, wherein Abu Ayyūb Al-Ansārī ﷺ narrates that the Holy Prophet ﷺ said:

'Whoever recites the *Ayah-al-Kursī* [2:255] and the ayah '*shahid-Allāhu*' [3:18] and '*Qulillāhumma-mālikalmulki*' until '*bighayrihisāb*' [3:26-27], Allāh Ta'ālā will forgive all his sins, admit him into Paradise, and take care of seventy [i.e. plenty] of his needs, the simplest of these being His forgiveness.' [122]

Furthermore, in a hadīth reported by Īmām al Baghawī ﷴ, the Holy Prophet ﷺ is said to have stated:

'It is Allāh's promise that anyone who recites, after every salāh, Sūrah Fātiha, the *Ayah-al-Kursī*, and two verses of Āl Imrān, that is '*shahid-Allāhu*' [3:18] and the present verse: '*Qulillāhumma-mālikalmulki*' until '*bighayrihisāb*' [3:26-27], He will make his abode in Paradise, have him placed in the Sacred Enclosure, blessed with His mercy seventy times every day, fulfil seventy of his needs,

---

[121] Qur'ān 3:26-27.

[122] Shafi, Mufti Muhammad, Ma'ariful Qur'ān. Translated by Prof. Hasan Askari & Muhammad Taqi Usmani, Karachi: Maktaba Darul Uloom, Vol. 2, p. 43.

and protect him against every envier and enemy and make him prevail over them.' [123]

ELEVEN TIMES AFTER ISHĀ FOR BARAKAH IN RIZQ

It is the experience of the mashāikh that whosever recites these verses eleven times after Ishā salāh, Allāh ﷻ opens the doors of provision and sustenance for them. However, you must be constant upon it first and punctually recite them after Ishā every day to experience the full effect.

YAWM-AD-DEEN

The second part of this verse refers to 'Yawm-ad-Deen', i.e. 'the Day of Requital'. The word 'Yawm' itself carries three meanings here: that of the word's conventional usage, its definition according to Islamic legal language, and its intended meaning in this verse.

In conventional usage, the term 'Yawm' means 'day' – the period of time between sunrise and sunset. However, according to Islamic legal ruling, the day begins from the period of astronomical twilight [i.e. 'true dawn'] rather than sunrise, and ends at sunset, giving the legal day roughly two more hours than the normal one. This is why one can recite Sūrah Kahf or take a bath before sunrise on Friday and still gain the full reward of the sunnah practice, and why the Islamic definition of midday is an hour before the sun reaches its zenith.

The intended meaning here, however, is 'al-Yawm al-Ākhir', meaning the 'Last Day'. It is referred to as the 'Last Day' because it is the literal last day of this existence, as well as the literal first day of the existence of the Hereafter.

---

[123]Shafi, Mufti Muhammad, Ma'ariful Qur'ān. Translated by Prof. Hasan Askari & Muhammad Taqi Usmani, Karachi: Maktaba Darul Uloom, Vol. 2, p. 54.

THE BLOWING OF THE TRUMPET

Upon the 'Last Day', the trumpet [Sūr] will be blown and the Sun will implode and flicker out, the stars will swoop down and scatter, the sky will tear apart, the seas will flare up and burst forth, and the mountains will be torn from the earth and tumble through the sky like carded wool. No day will ever dawn again for this existence. Then a great period of time will pass in which nothing will exist. Except Allāh ﷻ alone:

$$ كُلُّ مَنْ عَلَيْهَا فَانٍ ۝ وَيَبْقَىٰ وَجْهُ رَبِّكَ ذُو الْجَلَالِ وَالْإِكْرَامِ ۝ $$

Everyone who is on it [the earth] has to perish. And the face [essence, zaat] of your Rabb will remain, the Lord of might and grace. [124]

And:

$$ وَلَا تَدْعُ مَعَ اللَّهِ إِلَٰهًا آخَرَ ۖ لَا إِلَٰهَ إِلَّا هُوَ ۚ $$

$$ كُلُّ شَيْءٍ هَالِكٌ إِلَّا وَجْهَهُ ۚ لَهُ الْحُكْمُ وَإِلَيْهِ تُرْجَعُونَ ۝ $$

And do not invoke any other god along with Allāh. There is no god but He. Everything is going to perish except His zaat. He alone has the right to judge, and to Him you are to be returned. [125]

After this period of forty or so years, the archangel Isrāfil ﷺ will be brought forth and he will blow the trumpet a second time, and everything will come into existence once more. Every living thing that ever existed will be given life again, and land will be stretched out to accommodate all. Mankind will arise from their graves:

$$ يَوْمَ يَخْرُجُونَ مِنَ الْأَجْدَاثِ سِرَاعًا كَأَنَّهُمْ إِلَىٰ نُصُبٍ يُوفِضُونَ ۝ $$

---

[124] Qur'ān 55:26-27
[125] Qur'ān 28:88.

خَاشِعَةً أَبْصَارُهُمْ تَرْهَقُهُمْ ذِلَّةٌ ۚ ذَٰلِكَ الْيَوْمُ الَّذِي كَانُوا يُوعَدُونَ ۞

The Day they [the mushrikeen] will come out of the graves quickly, as if they were rushing towards an idol, with their eyes downcast, disgrace will cover them. That is the Day, which they were being promised. [126]

The angels will call to them and drive them towards the plain of resurrection, the appointed place of gathering, of *Māhshar*. All will be gathered there and no one missed out:

لَّقَدْ أَحْصَاهُمْ وَعَدَّهُمْ عَدًّا ۞ وَكُلُّهُمْ آتِيهِ يَوْمَ الْقِيَامَةِ فَرْدًا ۞

He has fully encompassed them and precisely calculated their numbers, and each one of them is bound to come to Him on the Day of Judgement, all alone. [127]

Everyone from Adam ﷺ till the last man will all be there. Many will be in a wretched state. Naked and forlorn. The sun hammering down upon them. Despairing over lives of sin. In that condition of distress another forty years will pass. As the Arabic proverb says:

الانتظار اشد من الموت

For mankind, waiting is often worse than death. It is the nature of the human being that he becomes anxious and impatient and loses heart very quickly. It is the way he/she has been created. The human being cannot bear waiting, but on the Day of Qiyāmah, they will have to wait. Everyone will be standing in distress, saying to themselves that 'nothing is happening'. In the end, the distress and anxiety will become too much and they will begin to beseech each other to beg Allāh ﷻ to begin the Reckoning. And, in the words of Maulānā Ubaidullāh of Nizamuddin, every Hitler, Bitler, Hunter, Bunter, etc. will all proceed towards the Prophets ﷺ to plead on behalf of humanity for the

---

[126] Qur'ān 70:43-44.
[127] Qur'ān 19:94-95.

reckoning to commence. The famous ḥadīth of the Beloved Prophet's ﷺ intercession explains what will occur next in great detail. Abu Huraira ؓ relates that Messenger of Allāh ﷺ said:

I shall be the leader of mankind on the Day of Resurrection. Do you know why? Allāh will gather on one plain the earlier and the latter [people of the human race] on the Day of Resurrection. Then the voice of the proclaimer will be heard by all of them and the sight will penetrate through all of them and the sun will come near. People will then experience a degree of anguish, anxiety, and agony which they shall not be able to bear and they shall not be able to stand. Some people will say to the others, 'Don't you see in which trouble you are? Don't you see what [misfortune] has overtaken you? Why don't you find one who should intercede for you with your Rabb?' [And] Some will say to the others, 'Go to Adam [Ādam] عليه السلام.'

And they will go to Adam عليه السلام and say, 'O Adam عليه السلام, thou art the father of mankind. Allāh created thee by His own Hand, and breathed in thee of His spirit, and ordered the angels to prostrate before thee. Intercede for us with thy Rabb. Don't you see in what [trouble] we are? Don't you see what [misfortune] has overtaken us?

Adam عليه السلام will say:

إِنَّ رَبِّي قَدْ غَضِبَ الْيَوْمَ غَضَبًا لَمْ يَغْضَبْ قَبْلَهُ مِثْلَهُ وَلَنْ يَغْضَبَ بَعْدَهُ مِثْلَهُ وَإِنَّهُ نَهَانِي عَنِ الشَّجَرَةِ فَعَصَيْتُهُ نَفْسِي نَفْسِي اذْهَبُوا إِلَى غَيْرِي اذْهَبُوا إِلَى نُوحٍ

'Verily, my Rabb is angry this day, to an extent to which He has never been angry before, nor will He ever be after. Verily, He forbade me [to go near] that tree and I disobeyed Him. I am concerned for myself. Go to someone else; go to Noah [Nūḥ] عليه السلام.'

They will go to Noah عليه السلام and will say, 'O Noah عليه السلام, thou art the first of the Messengers [sent] on the earth [after Adam عليه السلام], and Allāh named thee as a "Grateful Servant", intercede for us with thy Rabb. Don't you see in what [trouble] we are? Don't you see what [misfortune] has overtaken us?'

He will reply to them:

إِنَّ رَبِّي قَدْ غَضِبَ الْيَوْمَ غَضَبًا لَمْ يَغْضَبْ قَبْلَهُ مِثْلَهُ وَلَنْ يَغْضَبَ بَعْدَهُ مِثْلَهُ وَإِنَّهُ قَدْ
كَانَتْ لِي دَعْوَةٌ دَعَوْتُ بِهَا عَلَى قَوْمِي نَفْسِي نَفْسِي اذْهَبُوا إِلَى إِبْرَاهِيمَ

'Verily, my Rabb is angry this day, to an extent to which He has never been angry
before, nor will He ever be after. There has emanated a curse from me with which I
cursed my people. I am concerned for myself, I am concerned for myself. You should
go to Ibrāhīm ﷺ.'

They will go to Ibrāhīm ﷺ and say, 'Thou art the apostle of Allāh and His
Friend amongst the inhabitants of the earth; intercede for us with thy Rabb.
Don't you see in which [trouble] we are? Don't you see what [misfortune] has
overtaken us?'

Ibrāhīm ﷺ will say to them:

إِنَّ رَبِّي قَدْ غَضِبَ الْيَوْمَ غَضَبًا لَمْ يَغْضَبْ قَبْلَهُ مِثْلَهُ وَلَنْ يَغْضَبَ بَعْدَهُ مِثْلَهُ

'Verily, my Rabb is angry this day, to an extent to which He has never been angry
before, nor will He ever be after.' And [Ibrāhīm ﷺ] will mention his lies [128] *[and then*

---

[128] These are the three occasions on which Ibrāhīm ﷺ said something, but meant a
different meaning to the one commonly used. This is known as *Tawriya* and is not
actually lying, but rather making an ambiguous allusion or using a word with a double
meaning. The three occasions are mentioned in the following aḥadīth: Abu Hurairah
ﷺ reported the Prophet ﷺ as saying, 'Ibrāhīm ﷺ never told a lie except on three
occasions – twice for the sake of Allāh. Allāh quoted his words [in the Qur'ān] "I am
indeed sick" and "Rather, this is done by this chief of theirs." And the third was when
Abraham passed through the land of a tyrant [king] and [his wife] Sara was
accompanying him. He stayed there in a place. People went to the tyrant and informed
him saying, "A man has come down here; he has a most beautiful woman with him." So

say],'I am concerned for myself, I am concerned for myself. You should go to someone else: go to Moses ﷺ.

They will come to Moses ﷺ and say: O Moses, thou art Allāh's messenger, Allāh blessed thee with His messenger-ship and His conversation among people. Intercede for us with thy Rabb. Don't you see in what [trouble] we are? Don't you see what [misfortune] has overtaken us?'

Moses ﷺ will say to them:

إِنَّ رَبِّي قَدْ غَضِبَ الْيَوْمَ غَضَبًا لَمْ يَغْضَبْ قَبْلَهُ مِثْلَهُ وَلَنْ يَغْضَبَ بَعْدَهُ مِثْلَهُ وَإِنِّي قَتَلْتُ نَفْسًا لَمْ أُومَرْ بِقَتْلِهَا نَفْسِي نَفْسِي اذْهَبُوا إِلَى عِيسَى

'Verily, my Rabb is angry this day, to an extent to which He has never been angry before, nor will He ever be after. And I, in fact, killed a person whom I had not been ordered to kill. I am concerned for myself, I am concerned for myself. You should go to Jesus ﷺ.'

They will come to Jesus ﷺ and will say, 'O Jesus ﷺ, thou art the messenger of Allāh and thou conversed with people in the cradle, [thou art] His Word which He sent down upon Mary and [thou art] the Spirit from Him; so intercede for us with thy Rabb. Don't you see [the trouble] in which we are? Don't you see [the misfortune] that has overtaken us?'

Jesus ﷺ will say:

---

he [the king] sent for him [Ibrāhīm] and asked about her. He said she is my sister. When he returned to her, he said, "He asked me about you and I informed him that you were my sister. Today there is no believer except me and you. You are my sister in the Book of Allāh [i.e. sister in faith]. So do not belie me before him.' [Bukhārī: 3358, 5084; Abu Dāwūd: 2212]. The Hadīth continues. Allāh saved her from the tyrant.

إِنَّ رَبِّي قَدْ غَضِبَ الْيَوْمَ غَضَبًا لَمْ يَغْضَبْ قَبْلَهُ مِثْلَهُ وَلَنْ يَغْضَبَ بَعْدَهُ مِثْلَهُ — وَلَمْ يَذْكُرْ لَهُ ذَنْبًا — نَفْسِي نَفْسِي اذْهَبُوا إِلَى غَيْرِي اذْهَبُوا إِلَى مُحَمَّدٍ

"Verily, my Rabb is angry this day, to an extent to which He has never been angry before, nor will He ever be after. [He ﷻ mentioned no sin of his] I am concerned for myself, I am concerned for myself. Go to someone else. Go to Muhammad ﷺ.' [129]

And so they will come to me [i.e. the Prophet ﷺ] and say, 'O Muhammad ﷺ, thou art the messenger of Allāh and the last of the apostles. Allāh has pardoned thee all thy previous and later sins. Intercede for us with thy Rabb; don't you see in which [trouble] we are? Don't you see what [misfortune] has overtaken us?' They will come to me and I will say:

أنا لها أنا لها أنا لها

'This is my duty, this is my duty.'

I shall then set off and come below the Throne and fall down in prostration before my Rabb; then Allāh will reveal to me and inspire me with some of His Praises and Glorifications, which He has not revealed to anyone before me. He will then say:

يا محمد ارفع رأسك وسل تعطه واشفع تشفع

*'Muhammad ﷺ, raise thy head. Ask and it will be granted.
Intercede, and thy intercession will be accepted.'*

'I will then raise my head and say, 'O my Rabb, my people, my people.'

It will be said, 'O Muhammad ﷺ, bring in by the right gate of Paradise [exclusively] those of your people who will have no account to render. And [as for the others] they will share with the people the other doors besides this

---

[129] A servant who has had his previous and later sins all forgiven.

door.' The Prophet ﷺ then said: By Him in Whose Hand is the life of Muhammad ﷺ, verily the distance between two door leaves of Paradise is as great as between Mecca and Hajar, or as between Mecca and Busra. [130]

And so the reckoning will finally commence, and Allāh ﷻ will order the angels to descend:

$$\text{وَيَوْمَ تَشَقَّقُ السَّمَاءُ بِالْغَمَامِ وَنُزِّلَ الْمَلَائِكَةُ تَنزِيلًا ۝}$$

$$\text{الْمُلْكُ يَوْمَئِذٍ الْحَقُّ لِلرَّحْمَٰنِ ۚ وَكَانَ يَوْمًا عَلَى الْكَافِرِينَ عَسِيرًا ۝}$$

The Day the sky will break open with the clouds, and the angels will be sent down in a majestic descent. The Kingdom on that day will be for Raḥmān [the All-Merciful, Allāh], and it will be a difficult day for the disbelievers. [131]

And:

$$\text{كَلَّا إِذَا دُكَّتِ الْأَرْضُ دَكًّا دَكًّا ۝ وَجَاءَ رَبُّكَ وَالْمَلَكُ صَفًّا صَفًّا ۝}$$

$$\text{وَجِيءَ يَوْمَئِذٍ بِجَهَنَّمَ ۚ يَوْمَئِذٍ يَتَذَكَّرُ الْإِنسَانُ وَأَنَّىٰ لَهُ الذِّكْرَىٰ ۝}$$

No! When the earth will be crushed thoroughly to be turned into bits, and your Rabb will come, and the angels as well, lined up in rows, and Jahannam [Hell], on that day, will be brought forward, it will be the day when man will realise the truth, but from where will he take advantage of such realisation? [132]

The heavens will tear open and all the angels will come down row upon row, and at that time the eyesight of the people will become very sharp and they will see everything: the skies ripping open and the angels descending. Now the

---

[130] Bukhārī: 3340, 4476, 7410, 7440, 7510; Muslim: 194a, 194b.

[131] Qur'ān 25:25-26.

[132] Qur'ān 89:21-23.

earth will be crowded with angels, surrounding all of creation. And then Allāh ﷻ will descend [as it befits His Majesty] and judgement will begin.

There will be a proper judiciary court, and the reckoning will be done in a formal way just as it is done in this world. First, a person will be taken to account regarding his salāh, then zakāt, fasts, and Hajj. And the first thing to be taken to account in regards to Huqooqul Ibadd [rights of fellow human beings] will be regarding blood. If a person shed someone's blood, killed someone, stabbed someone, or injured someone, regardless of whether the blood was one bucket full, or one glass full, or just a few drops were shed, he will face severe questioning.

Abuse, insult, and dishonouring, belittling someone, putting someone down, backbiting someone, casting accusations on someone: all will be accounted for. And there will be a lot of commotion, turmoil and confusion at that time.

The disbelievers will be separated from those who believed. It will be said [to the angels] take them to the hellfire. Jahannam will be brought closer and so will Jannah. Abu Hurairah ﷺ narrates that the Messenger of Allāh ﷺ said:

'Some of the Fire [in the shape of a long neck] will come out of the Fire on the Day of Judgement. It will have two eyes which can see, two ears which can hear, and a tongue which can speak. It will say:

إِنِّي وُكِّلْتُ بِثَلَاثَةٍ بِكُلِّ جَبَّارٍ عَنِيدٍ وَبِكُلِّ

مَنْ دَعَا مَعَ اللَّهِ إِلَهًا آخَرَ وَبِالْمُصَوِّرِينَ

"I have been put in charge of three: every obstinate oppressor,
everyone who called upon a deity besides Allāh, and the image makers.'" [133]

And it will take them, the oppressors, the corrupt, the wicked, the rebellious, and the mischievous, and pull them into the hellfire. They will be flung from the top of Jahannam. They will attempt to resist, refuse to go, but the angels

---

[133] Tirmīdhī, 39: 2775.

will take them, drag them by their forelocks and by their legs, and they will be thrown into the fire.

$$ يُعْرَفُ الْمُجْرِمُونَ بِسِيمَاهُمْ فَيُؤْخَذُ بِالنَّوَاصِي وَالْأَقْدَامِ ۞ $$

The guilty ones will be recognised through
their marks and will be seized by foreheads and feet. [134]

And the reckoning will continue. Those who are sinless, those whose sins have all been forgiven, Allāh ﷻ will say they have no account to give. They left the world just the way they entered it: they came into the world with nothing and left with nothing. It will be said that take them and enter them straight into Paradise.

Shāh Abdur-Rahīm Raipūrī ◌ used to distribute all his belongings amongst the poor and destitute. When he passed away he had no house, as he used to stay in the khānqāh which was waqf and whatever money he had for food and drink he would distribute. He would ask his khādim-e-khās Shāh Abdul Qādir Raipūrī ◌ to let him borrow a pair of clothes. He gave all his clothes away in charity. When he passed away he didn't own one penny, nor did he owe any person anything. He left the world in the same way in which he entered the world from the womb of his mother; owning nothing.

We have the whole world, it's going to be difficult to give account of everything. This is why this day will become very long for some and very short for others, such people like Shāh Abdur-Rahīm Raipūrī ◌, whose reckoning will be over in seconds. For some it will last a thousand years:

$$ وَيَسْتَعْجِلُونَكَ بِالْعَذَابِ وَلَن يُخْلِفَ اللَّهُ وَعْدَهُ ۚ $$

$$ وَإِنَّ يَوْمًا عِندَ رَبِّكَ كَأَلْفِ سَنَةٍ مِّمَّا تَعُدُّونَ ۞ $$

---

[134] Qur'ān 55:41.

They ask you to bring the punishment sooner, while Allāh will never go back on His promise. In fact, one day with your Rabb is like one thousand years according to your calculation. [135]

For others, it will last fifty thousand years:

$$مِّنَ اللَّهِ ذِي الْمَعَارِجِ ۝ تَعْرُجُ الْمَلَائِكَةُ وَالرُّوحُ إِلَيْهِ$$

$$فِي يَوْمٍ كَانَ مِقْدَارُهُ خَمْسِينَ أَلْفَ سَنَةٍ ۝$$

[And it will come] from Allāh, the Rabb of the stairways, to whom ascend the angels and the Spirit in a day the length of which is fifty thousand years. [136]

The Day of Requital is the Day of Judgement, Justice, and Recompense. It is the day that will make clear distinction between Haqq and Baatil [truth and falsehood]. It is the day when accounts will be taken and everyone will be given their due. It is stated in a Hadīth that on the Day of Judgement, in every person's book of deeds, there will be a list of three kinds of deeds: one list will have deeds out of which Allāh ﷻ will not forgive even a word, and this would include Shirk [idolatry] and Kufr [disbelief]. In the second list will be deeds about which Allāh ﷻ won't bother, these will be the sins which man would have committed against his own self [i.e. matters between Allāh ﷻ and the man, for example somebody did not fast, neglected prayers]. If Allāh ﷻ wills, He could forgive. In the third list will be the deeds Allāh ﷻ will not interfere, which includes violating the rights of fellow human beings. [137]

As for the first list, that of idolatry and disbelief, those are the people regarding whom Allāh ﷻ tells us:

---

[135] Qur'ān 22:47.

[136] Qur'ān 70:3-4.

[137] Musnad Ahmed.

وَامْتَازُوا الْيَوْمَ أَيُّهَا الْمُجْرِمُونَ ۝ أَلَمْ أَعْهَدْ إِلَيْكُمْ يَا بَنِي آدَمَ أَن لَّا تَعْبُدُوا

الشَّيْطَانَ ۚ إِنَّهُ لَكُمْ عَدُوٌّ مُّبِينٌ ۝ وَأَنِ اعْبُدُونِي ۚ هَٰذَا صِرَاطٌ مُّسْتَقِيمٌ ۝ وَلَقَدْ

أَضَلَّ مِنكُمْ جِبِلًّا كَثِيرًا ۖ أَفَلَمْ تَكُونُوا تَعْقِلُونَ ۝ هَٰذِهِ جَهَنَّمُ الَّتِي كُنتُمْ تُوعَدُونَ ۝

اصْلَوْهَا الْيَوْمَ بِمَا كُنتُمْ تَكْفُرُونَ ۝

*And [it will be said to the infidels,] "Separate yourselves today O the guilty ones! Did I
not direct you, O children of 'Ādam [Adam], that you must not worship the Satan,
[because] he is an open enemy for you, and that you must worship Me, [because] this
is the straight path? He had misguided many people from among you. So, did you not
have sense? [Now] This is the Jahannam of which you were consistently warned. Enter
it today, because you have been persistently denying [the truth]."* [138]

We should pray constantly for a good death upon Īmān. So many cases have
been witnessed, where a man believed and did good works during his life but
through some objections lost his faith before the end, dooming himself for
eternity. May Allāh ﷻ protect us and protect our future generations.

رَبَّنَا لَا تُزِغْ قُلُوبَنَا بَعْدَ إِذْ هَدَيْتَنَا وَهَبْ لَنَا

مِن لَّدُنكَ رَحْمَةً ۚ إِنَّكَ أَنتَ الْوَهَّابُ ۝

*Our Rabb, do not let our hearts deviate from the right path after You have given us
guidance, and bestow upon us mercy from Yourself. Surely, You, and You alone, are
the One who bestows in abundance.* [139]

The second list regards the rights of Allāh ﷻ over us. It is Allāh's ﷻ divine right
that we worship Him alone, pray our salāh, pay our zakāh, fast, make

---

pilgrimage, dhikr and recite Qur'ān. We should also avoid disobedience like zinā, drinking, drugs, and all other harām actions. Allāh ﷻ may be lenient in this and forgive whoever He wills. Without doubt He is the Most Compassionate and the Most Merciful, yet we should not rely on this forgiveness breaking His supreme commands, for there is no guarantee that we will be amongst the ones forgiven. This mercy and forgiveness comes as a special result of some deeds that a person may have performed during a certain state in his/her life, in lieu of which Allāh ﷻ will forgive that persons misdeeds. Abu Huraira ﷺ reports Allāh's Messenger ﷺ as having said:

There was a dog wandering around a well whom thirst would have killed. Suddenly a prostitute from the prostitutes of Bani Isrā'il happened to see it and she drew water in her shoe and made it drink, and she was pardoned because of this. [140] Yet, the general rule is that one will be held to account for this list as well.

The third and final list will be regarding the rights of people, meaning how people have interacted with each other. As a general rule, Allāh ﷻ will not interfere in this list nor show leniency or flexibility, as is explained in the Hadīth known as the 'Hadīth of Muflis'.

THE HADĪTH OF MUFLIS

Abu Huraira ﷺ reported Allāh's Messenger ﷺ as saying: Do you know who is poor? They [the Companions] said: 'A poor man amongst us is one who has neither dirham nor property.' He ﷺ said: 'The poor of my Ummah would be he who would come on the Day of Resurrection with prayers and fasts and zakāh but [he would find himself bankrupt on that day, as he would have exhausted his funds of virtues] since he had hurled abuses upon others, brought calumny against others and unlawfully consumed the wealth of others and shed the blood of others and beat others, his virtues would be credited to

---

[140] Muslim: 2245 b, 1567 a.

the account of those [who suffered at his hand]. And if his good deeds fall short to clear the account, then their sins would be placed on him, and he would be thrown in the Hell-Fire.' [141] In very few cases, Allāh ﷻ will intervene and grant the wronged party some reward in lieu of the person. But this will be very rare, so we should be very careful in our dealings with people. May Allāh ﷻ protect us!

THE WEIGHING IN THE SCALES

After this, the deeds will be weighed in the Scale:

وَالْوَزْنُ يَوْمَئِذٍ الْحَقُّ ۚ فَمَن ثَقُلَتْ مَوَازِينُهُ فَأُولَٰئِكَ هُمُ الْمُفْلِحُونَ ۞ وَمَنْ خَفَّتْ مَوَازِينُهُ فَأُولَٰئِكَ الَّذِينَ خَسِرُوا أَنفُسَهُم بِمَا كَانُوا بِآيَاتِنَا يَظْلِمُونَ ۞

The Weighing [of deeds] on that day is definite. As for those whose scales are heavy, they will be the successful ones. But those whose scales are light, they are the ones who have brought loss to themselves, because they used to be unjust to our commands. [142]

And:

وَنَضَعُ الْمَوَازِينَ الْقِسْطَ لِيَوْمِ الْقِيَامَةِ فَلَا تُظْلَمُ نَفْسٌ شَيْئًا ۖ وَإِن كَانَ مِثْقَالَ حَبَّةٍ مِّنْ خَرْدَلٍ أَتَيْنَا بِهَا ۗ وَكَفَىٰ بِنَا حَاسِبِينَ ۞

We shall place scales to do justice on the Day of Judgement. So no one shall be wronged in the least. Even if it [a deed] is to the measure of a mustard seed, We will bring it forth, and We are enough to take account. [143]

---

[141] Muslim: 2581.

[142] Qur'ān 7:8-9.

[143] Qur'ān 21:47.

THE SIZE OF THE SCALES

Regarding the size of the scale, a Hadīth is narrated in which it is stated that the balance will be set up on the Day of Resurrection, and if the heavens and the Earth were to be weighed in it, it would be sufficient to carry them. And the angels will say, 'O Rabb, who is this for?' Allāh ﷻ will say, 'For whomsoever I will from among My slaves'. [144] The deeds will be weighed and those with much good and few bad deeds will be shown leniency and their bad deeds will be forgiven or even replaced with good. As for those whose bad deeds far outweigh the good, they will be cast into the Fire, until they are cleansed and purified, before being admitted into Jannah. There will also be those whose good deeds and bad deeds are at a balance, and will be in need of a single deed to tip the balance in their favour. They will look to kith and kin for the gift of a single deed, but all will turn away from them and flee:

فَإِذَا جَاءَتِ الصَّاخَّةُ ۞ يَوْمَ يَفِرُّ الْمَرْءُ مِنْ أَخِيهِ ۞ وَأُمِّهِ وَأَبِيهِ ۞ وَصَاحِبَتِهِ وَبَنِيهِ ۞ لِكُلِّ امْرِئٍ مِّنْهُمْ يَوْمَئِذٍ شَأْنٌ يُغْنِيهِ ۞

So when the Deafening Noise will occur, the Day when one will flee from his brother, and from his mother and father, and from his wife and sons, every one of them will be too engaged in his own affairs to care for others. [145]

A'RĀF

Such people will be sent to a place called A'rāf, a bridge between Heaven and Hell from where they will watch proceedings until Judgement is completed,

---

[144] al-Silsilāt al-Sahīhah, 941.
[145] Qur'ān 80:33-37.

fretting over his/her fate. Then Allāh ﷻ will enter these people into Jannah as well, through His infinite mercy.

INTENDING TO DO GOOD IS ALSO A HASANAH

Therefore, we should increase our good actions and rectify our intentions. Abu Huraira ﷺ narrates that Allāh's Messenger ﷺ said, "Allāh says, 'If My slave intends to do a bad deed then [O Angels] do not write it unless he does it; if he does it, then write it as it is, but if he, for My sake, refrains from doing it, then write it as a good deed [in his account]. [On the other hand] if he intends to do a good deed, but does not do it, then write a good deed [in his account], and if he does it, then write it for him [in his account] as ten good deeds up to seven-hundred times.'" [146]

How unfortunate is the one whose bad deeds outweigh his good deeds, when 'Allāh would even wipe out [the evil committed by man] and no one is put to destruction except he who is a real loser. [147]

EXAMINING THE BOOKS

Amongst these people will be those whose books of deeds will be examined by the Angels, by Allāh's ﷻ command. The Mother of the Believers, 'A'isha ﷺ reported that Allāh's Messenger ﷺ said:

He who is taken to account on the Day of Resurrection is in fact put to torment. I said: Has Allāh, the Exalted and Glorious, not said this: 'He will be made subject to an easy reckoning'? [148] Thereupon he said: [What it implies]

---

[146] al-Bukhārī: 6491, 7501.
[147] Muslim 131 b.
[148] Qur'ān 84:8.

is not the actual reckoning, but only the presentation of one's deeds to Him. He who is thoroughly examined in reckoning is put to torment. [149]

One is to flick through the accounts, and the other is to examine them thoroughly and ask questions. When one's accounts are just flicked through, he/she will be let off easily. However, if scrutiny starts, then one will be doomed. May Allāh ﷻ save us from severe questioning.

RESULTS BEING HANDED OUT

Then the certificates of our results will be given out. Those who pass will receive their certificates in their right hands. Those who fail will receive their certificates in their left hands behind their backs, in shame. Allāh ﷻ says:

وَأَمَّا مَنْ أُوتِيَ كِتَابَهُ بِشِمَالِهِ فَيَقُولُ يَا لَيْتَنِي لَمْ أُوتَ كِتَابِيَهْ ۞ وَلَمْ أَدْرِ مَا حِسَابِيَهْ ۞

يَا لَيْتَهَا كَانَتِ الْقَاضِيَةَ ۞ مَا أَغْنَىٰ عَنِّي مَالِيَهْ ۛ هَلَكَ عَنِّي سُلْطَانِيَهْ ۞

As for him who will be given his book in his left hand, he will say, "Oh, would that I had not been given my book, and I had never known what my account is! Oh, would that it [death] had been the end of the matter! My wealth has not been of any use to me. My power has gone from me for good". [150]

And:

وَأَمَّا مَنْ أُوتِيَ كِتَابَهُ وَرَاءَ ظَهْرِهِ ۞ فَسَوْفَ يَدْعُو ثُبُورًا ۞ وَيَصْلَىٰ سَعِيرًا ۞

As for the one whose book [of deeds] will be given to him from behind his back, he will pray for death, but he will enter the blazing fire. [151]

---

[149] Muslim: 2876 a, Abu Dāwūd: 3093.

[150] Qur'ān 69:25-29.

[151] Qur'ān 84:10-12.

And:

$$كُلُّ نَفْسٍ ذَائِقَةُ الْمَوْتِ ۗ وَإِنَّمَا تُوَفَّوْنَ أُجُورَكُمْ يَوْمَ الْقِيَامَةِ ۖ فَمَن زُحْزِحَ$$

$$عَنِ النَّارِ وَأُدْخِلَ الْجَنَّةَ فَقَدْ فَازَ ۗ وَمَا الْحَيَاةُ الدُّنْيَا إِلَّا مَتَاعُ الْغُرُورِ$$

*Every soul has to taste death. It is on the Day of Judgement that you shall be paid your
rewards in full. So, whoever has been kept away from the Fire and admitted to
Paradise has really succeeded. The worldly life is nothing but an illusionary
enjoyment.* [152]

And:

$$فَأَمَّا مَنْ أُوتِيَ كِتَابَهُ بِيَمِينِهِ فَيَقُولُ هَاؤُمُ اقْرَءُوا كِتَابِيَهْ ۞ إِنِّي ظَنَنتُ أَنِّي مُلَاقٍ حِسَابِيَهْ$$

$$۞ فَهُوَ فِي عِيشَةٍ رَّاضِيَةٍ ۞ فِي جَنَّةٍ عَالِيَةٍ ۞ قُطُوفُهَا دَانِيَةٌ ۞ كُلُوا وَاشْرَبُوا هَنِيئًا بِمَا$$

$$أَسْلَفْتُمْ فِي الْأَيَّامِ الْخَالِيَةِ ۞$$

*Now, as for him who is given his book in his right hand, he will say [to his colleagues],
"Come here, read my book. I was sure that I would encounter my reckoning." So he
will be in a well-pleasing life in a lofty garden, the fruits of which will be close at hand.
[It will be said to such people,] "Eat and drink with pleasure, as a reward for what you
did in advance during past days".* [153]

This will all happen on that Day of Recompense. We pray that Allāh ﷻ makes
our path easy for us, tips the Scale in our favour, saves us from a hard
reckoning, and grants that we receive our books in our right hands.

---

[152] Qur'ān 3:185.

[153] Qur'ān 69:19-24

HELL DRAWN CLOSER TO MAYDAANE HASHR

Hell will also be brought close to the Plain of Judgement, as Abdullāh bin Mas'ūd ﷺ narrates that the Messenger of Allāh ﷺ said:

'Hell will be brought forth on that Day [of Resurrection] having seventy thousand bridles, and with every handle will be seventy thousand angels dragging it.' [154]

It will surround the Plain from all sides, like a vast ocean surrounding an island. There will be only one means of crossing this great terror: the Bridge of Sirāt [Pul-Sirāt]. Surrounded by a fully uncovered Jahannam, with only one means to cross, as the Qur'ān states:

$$وَأُزْلِفَتِ الْجَنَّةُ لِلْمُتَّقِينَ ۞ وَبُرِّزَتِ الْجَحِيمُ لِلْغَاوِينَ ۞$$

And the Paradise will be brought near to the God-fearing,
and the Hell will be fully uncovered for the perverse. [155]

And:

$$فَإِذَا جَاءَتِ الطَّامَّةُ الْكُبْرَىٰ ۞ يَوْمَ يَتَذَكَّرُ الْإِنسَانُ مَا سَعَىٰ ۞ وَبُرِّزَتِ الْجَحِيمُ لِمَن يَرَىٰ ۞ فَأَمَّا مَن طَغَىٰ ۞ وَآثَرَ الْحَيَاةَ الدُّنْيَا ۞ فَإِنَّ الْجَحِيمَ هِيَ الْمَأْوَىٰ ۞ وَأَمَّا مَنْ خَافَ مَقَامَ رَبِّهِ وَنَهَى النَّفْسَ عَنِ الْهَوَىٰ ۞ فَإِنَّ الْجَنَّةَ هِيَ الْمَأْوَىٰ ۞$$

So when the Greatest Havoc will take place on the day when man will recall what he did, and the Hell will be exposed for all who see, then for the one who had rebelled, and preferred the worldly life [to the Hereafter], the Hell will be the abode, whereas

---

[154] Muslim: 2842
[155] Qur'ān 26:90-91.

for the one who feared to stand before his Rabb, and restrained his self from the [evil] desire, the Paradise will be the abode. [156]

TWO ACTIONS THAT WILL HELP US IN CROSSING OVER JAHANNAM

A persons good deeds will help him cross over the bridge, especially two things: [1] Trustworthiness and honesty in dealing with each other, and, [2] The keeping of ties and relations with kith and kin.

As the crossing begins, a darkness will pass over the procession. The only light visible to a person will emanate from the good deeds he did. The more good a person did, the more the light; the less good a person did, the less will be his/her light. People will be making duā:

$$رَبَّنَا أَتْمِمْ لَنَا نُورَنَا وَاغْفِرْ لَنَا ۖ$$

$$إِنَّكَ عَلَىٰ كُلِّ شَيْءٍ قَدِيرٌ ۞$$

*"O our Rabb! Complete our Nūr for us and
forgive us, for you have power over everything."* [157]

Some will be full of nūr while others will have nūr equivalent to their finger nails.

THE HADĪTH REGARDING THE CROSSING OVER THE BRIDGE

Abu Huraira ؓ narrates that some people asked:

"O Allāh's Messenger ﷺ! Shall we see our Rabb on the Day of Resurrection?" He ﷺ said, "Do you crowd and squeeze each other on looking at the sun

---

[156] Qur'ān 79:34-41.
[157] Qur'ān 66:8.

when it is not hidden by clouds?" They replied, "No, Allāh's Messenger ﷺ."
He ﷺ said, "Do you crowd and squeeze each other on looking at the moon
when it is full and not hidden by clouds?" They replied, 'No, O Allāh's
Messenger ﷺ!' He said, "So will you see Him on the Day of Resurrection.'
Allāh will gather all the people and say, 'Whoever used to worship anything
should follow that thing.' So, he who used to worship the sun, will follow it,
and he who used to worship the moon will follow it, and he who used to
worship false deities will follow them; and then only this nation [the
Muslims] will remain, including their hypocrites. Allāh will approach them in
a form other than what they know and will say, 'I am your Rabb.' They will
say, 'We seek refuge with Allāh from you. This is our place [and we will not
follow you] till our Rabb comes to us, and when our Rabb comes to us, we will
recognize Him. Then Allāh will approach them in a form which they know
and will say, "I am your Rabb.' They will say, '[No doubt] You are our Rabb,'
and they will follow Him [i.e. His instruction]. Then a bridge will be laid over
the [Hell] Fire." Allāh's Messenger ﷺ added, "I will be the first to cross it.
And the invocation of the Apostles on that Day, will be 'Allāhumma Sallim,
Sallim [O Allāh, save us, save us!].' And over that bridge there will be hooks
similar to the thorns of As-Sa'dān [a thorny tree]. Have you seen the thorns
of As-Sa'dān?" The companions said, "Yes, O Allāh's Messenger ﷺ." He ﷺ
added, "So the hooks over that bridge will be like the thorns of As-Sa'dān
except that their greatness in size is known only to Allāh. These hooks will
snatch the people according to their bad deeds. Some people will be ruined
because of their evil deeds, and some will be cut and injured and fall down in
Hell, but will be saved afterwards. When Allāh has finished the judgements
among His slaves, and intends to take out of the Fire whoever He wishes to
take out from among those who used to testify that none had the right to be
worshipped but Allāh, He will order the angels to take them out and the
angels will know them by the mark of the traces of prostration [on their
foreheads] for Allāh has banned the fire to consume the traces of prostration

on the body of Adam's son. So they will take them out, and by then they would have burnt [as coal], and then water, called the Mā-ul-Hayāt [Water of Life] will be poured over them, and they will spring out like a seed springs out on the bank of a rainwater stream, and there will remain one man who will be facing the [Hell] Fire and will say, 'O Rabb! It's [Hell's] vapours have poisoned and smoked me and its flame have burnt me. Please turn my face away from the Fire.' He will keep on invoking Allāh till Allāh says, 'Perhaps, if I give you what you want, you will ask for another thing?' The man will say, 'No, by Your Power, I will not ask You for anything else.' Then Allāh will turn his face away from the Fire. The man will say after that, 'O Rabb, bring me near the gate of Paradise.' Allāh will say [to him], 'Didn't you promise not to ask for anything else? Woe to you, O son of Adam! How treacherous you are!' The man will keep on invoking Allāh till Allāh will say, 'But if I give you that, you may ask me for something else.' The man will say, 'No, by Your Power. I will not ask for anything else.' He will give Allāh his covenant and promise not to ask for anything else after that. So Allāh will bring him near to the gate of Paradise, and when he sees what is in it, he will remain silent as long as Allāh wills, and then he will say, 'O Rabb! Let me enter Paradise.' Allāh will say, 'Didn't you promise that you would not ask Me for anything other than that? Woe to you, O son of Adam! How treacherous you are!' On that, the man will say, 'O Rabb! Do not make me the most wretched of Your creation,' and will keep on invoking Allāh till Allāh will smile. And when Allāh will smile because of him, He will then allow him to enter Paradise, and when he will enter Paradise, he will be addressed, 'Wish from so-and-so.' He will wish till all his wishes will be fulfilled, then Allāh will say, 'All this [i.e. what you have wished for] and as much again therewith are for you.' Abu Huraira ﷺ adds: That man will be the last of the people of Paradise to enter [Paradise]. [158]

---

[158] Bukhārī: 6573, 7437, 7438 & Muslim: 191 a.

THE SPEED OF CROSSING OVER THE BRIDGE

Some will pass over the Bridge in the blink of an eye, some at the speed of lightning, some as fast as the wind, some at the speed of a racing horse. Others will proceed at the pace of a running camel, some at the pace of regular men, while others slipping and faltering and crawling, feeling the extreme heat. The unfortunate ones will be overburdened by their bad deeds and cut and injured, falling into the flames below. These will be believers, [not non-believers], men and women whose wrongful deeds shall push them down into Jahannam. There will be many unfortunate ones. May Allāh 🕮 protect us! Once we have crossed, inshā'Allāh, the people will wait at the other side for everyone to reach. Meanwhile, the Beloved Messenger 🕮 will be racing back and forth saving as many from his Ummah as he can, as ibn al-Qayyim 🕮 records in a long hadīth related by Abdur-Rahman bin Samura 🕮 which states:

'. . . And I saw a man from my Ummah crawling on the Bridge [over the hell-fire] – sometimes crawling on it and sometimes clinging to it, when all of a sudden came his salawaat [prayers upon the Prophet 🕮] and raised him to his feet and rescued him.' [159]

THE WATER OF HAWDHE KAUTHAR

'Having been given from the Hawdh before judgement began, the Ummah will feel no thirst. Sahl bin Sa'd 🕮 reports that 'I heard Allāh's Apostle 🕮 as saying: I shall go to the Cistern before you and he who comes would drink and he who drinks would never feel thirsty, and there would come to me people whom I would know and who would know me. Then there would be intervention between me and them. Abu Hazim 🕮 said that Nu'man bin. Abu 'Ayyash 🕮 heard it and I narrated to them this hadīth, and said: Is it this that you heard Sahl 🕮 saying? He said: Yes, and I bear witness to the fact that I

---

[159] Mu'jamul Kabīr, Nawādirul Usul, Musnadul Firdaws, At-Targhib of Abu Mūsā.

heard it from Abu Sa'id Khudri ﷺ also, but he made this addition that he ﷺ would say: They are my followers, and it would be said to him: You do not know what they did after you and I will say to them: Woe to him who had changed [his religion] after me'. [160]

Entering into Jannah

Once the Ummah has crossed, the Beloved Prophet will lead them to the gates of Paradise. The Prophet ﷺ describes their size, stating, 'By Him in Whose Hand is the life of Muhammad ﷺ, verily the distance between the two door leaves of Paradise is as great as between Mecca and Hajar, or as between Mecca and Busra'. [161]

Moreover, Allāh ﷻ describes the scene of the believers upon entry into Jannah:

أُولَٰئِكَ لَهُمْ عُقْبَى الدَّارِ ۞ جَنَّاتُ عَدْنٍ يَدْخُلُونَهَا وَمَن صَلَحَ مِنْ آبَائِهِمْ وَأَزْوَاجِهِمْ وَذُرِّيَّاتِهِمْ ۖ وَالْمَلَائِكَةُ يَدْخُلُونَ عَلَيْهِم مِّن كُلِّ بَابٍ ۞ سَلَامٌ عَلَيْكُم بِمَا صَبَرْتُمْ ۚ فَنِعْمَ عُقْبَى الدَّارِ ۞

They are the ones for whom there is the ultimate abode, the eternal gardens they enter, and those as well who are righteous from their fathers, spouses, and progeny. The angels will enter onto them from every gate [saying], "Peace be upon you for the patience you observed. So, how excellent is the ultimate abode." [162]

And:

تَحِيَّتُهُمْ يَوْمَ يَلْقَوْنَهُ سَلَامٌ ۚ وَأَعَدَّ لَهُمْ أَجْرًا كَرِيمًا ۞

---

[160] Bukhārī: 6584, 7051 & Muslim 2290, 2291a, 249a.

[161] Muslim 194a, 194b.

[162] Qur'ān 13:22-24.

Their greeting, on the Day when they meet Him, will be, "Salām" [Peace]. And He has prepared for them a noble reward. [163]

And:

$$وَسِيقَ الَّذِينَ اتَّقَوْا رَبَّهُمْ إِلَى الْجَنَّةِ زُمَرًا ۖ حَتَّىٰ إِذَا جَاءُوهَا وَفُتِحَتْ أَبْوَابُهَا وَقَالَ لَهُمْ خَزَنَتُهَا سَلَامٌ عَلَيْكُمْ طِبْتُمْ فَادْخُلُوهَا خَالِدِينَ ۞$$

And those who used to fear their Rabb will be led towards Jannah [Paradise] in groups, until when they reach it, while its gates will be [already] opened [for them], and its keepers will say to them, "Salāmun-'alaikum [peace be on you]. How good are you! So, enter it to live here forever". [164]

The aḥādīth describe further the scene of Jannah. Thuwair ؓ narrates Ibn Umar ؓ as saying: The Messenger of Allāh ﷺ said:

"Indeed the least of the people of Paradise in rank is the one who shall look at his gardens, his wives, his bounties, his servants and his beds for the distance of a thousand years, and the noblest of them with Allāh is the one who shall look at His Face morning and night." Then the Messenger of Allāh ﷺ recited:

$$وُجُوهٌ يَوْمَئِذٍ نَّاضِرَةٌ ۞ إِلَىٰ رَبِّهَا نَاظِرَةٌ ۞$$

'Some faces on that day shall be radiant. They shall be looking at their Rabb.' [165]

Moreover, Abu Sa'eed Al-Khudri ؓ narrates that the Messenger of Allāh ﷺ said:

---

[163] Qur'ān 33:44.
[164] Qur'ān 39:73.
[165] Tirmīdhī.

"The least of the people of Paradise in position is the one with eighty thousand servants and seventy-two wives. He shall have a tent of pearl, peridot, and corundum set up for him, [the size of which is] like that which is between Al-Jabiyyah and Sana'a." [166]

And with the same chain, it is also narrated from the Prophet ﷺ that he said:

"Whoever of the people of [those destined to enter] Paradise dies, young or old, they shall be brought back in Paradise thirty years old, they will not increase in that ever, and likewise the people of the Fire." And with this chain, it is narrated from the Prophet ﷺ that he said: "There are upon them crowns, the least of its pearls would illuminate what is between the East and the West." [167]

THE HOSPITALITY UPON ENTERING JANNAH

The people of Jannah will be given a feast upon entry. Abu al-Sa'id Khudri ﷺ reports Allāh's Messenger ﷺ as saying that the earth would be turned into one single bread on the Day of Resurrection and the Almighty would turn it in His hand as one of you turns a loaf while on a journey. It would be a feast arranged in the honour of the people of Paradise. He [the narrator] further narrated that a person from among the Jews came and he said: Abu al-Qāsim ﷺ, may the Compassionate Rabb be pleased with you! May I inform you about the feast arranged in honour of the people of Paradise on the Day of Resurrection? He said: Do it, of course. He said: The earth would become one single bread. Then Allāh's Messenger ﷺ looked towards us and laughed until his molar teeth became visible. He then again said: May I inform you about that with which they would season it? He said: Do it, of course. He said: Their

---

[166] Mishkāt.
[167] Tirmīdhī.

seasoning would be bālām and fish. The Companions of the Prophet ﷺ said: What is this bālām? He said: Ox and fish from whose excess of the livers seventy thousand people would be able to eat. [168]

THE HOURIS OF JANNAH

What is more, waiting for the believers in Jannah will be the Houris. Their beauty is beyond worldly comprehension and described in hadīth thus:

'. . . A place in Paradise as small as the bow or whip of one of you is better than all the world and whatever is in it. And if a houri from Paradise appeared to the people of the earth, she would fill the space between Heaven and the Earth with light and pleasant scent. Her head cover is better than the world and whatever is in it. [169]

THE BEAUTY OF THE WOMEN OF THE WORLD

Despite their other worldly and awe-inspiring beauty, the Muslim women will be made even more beautiful, as is explained regarding the following verse:

كَذَٰلِكَ وَزَوَّجْنَاهُم بِحُورٍ عِينٍ ۝

Thus [it will happen,] and We will marry
them with houris having large dark eyes. [170]

Regarding this verse, Qurtubi ﵁ relates that Ibn Mubarak ﵁ mentions a narration that the human women who enter Paradise will be superior to the houris because of the good deeds they had performed upon the earth, and also

---

[168] Bukhārī: 6520 & Muslim: 2792.
[169] Bukhārī: 2796.
[170] Qur'ān 44:54.

an elevated [marfū'] hadīth stating, 'Human women [who enter Paradise] are seventy thousand times more superior than the houris'. [171] Indeed, many ahādīth corroborate this fact. The Mother of the Believers, Umm Salamah ﷠ narrates that she asked the Holy Prophet ﷺ, "O Rasūlullah ﷺ, are the women of this world superior or the houris [of Paradise]?" He ﷺ replied, "The women of this world will have superiority over the houris, just as the outer lining of a garment has superiority over the inner lining." Umm Salamah ﷠ then asked, "O Rasūlullah ﷺ, what is the reason for this?" He ﷺ answered, "Because they performed salāh, fasted, and worshipped. Allāh will put light on their faces and silk on their bodies. [The human women] will be fair in complexion and will wear green clothing and yellow jewellery. Their incense-burners will be made of pearls and their combs will be of gold. They will say, 'We are the women who will stay forever and we will never die. We are the women who will always remain in comfort and we will never undergo difficulty. We are the women who will stay and we will never leave. Listen, we are happy women and we will never become sad. Glad tidings to those men for whom we are and who are for us'". [172]

Furthermore Qurtubī ﷠ and Ibn Kathīr ﷠ both narrate that the houris will sing for their husbands, songs so marvellous that every hearer will be so pleased. The houris will intone: "We are houris, who have never sinned." The women of this world will reply to them saying: "We are the fasters [who kept fasts] and you are not, we are the prayers but you are not, and we are the givers of charity but you are not". [173]

Moreover, Abu Hurairah ﷠ narrates that Rasūlullāh ﷺ said:

"Every man in heaven will go to 72 of those created by Allāh [houris] and two of the women of mankind, these two women are superior to those created by

---

[171] Tafsīr Qurtubī.
[172] Tabrānī.
[173] al-Tadhkirah fī Aḥwāl al-Mawtá wa-Umūr al-Ākhirah & Al-Bidāya wa-n-nihāya.

Allāh [houris] with their worshipping [good deeds] they had performed in this world." [174]

IF A WOMAN HAD MARRIED MULTIPLE TIMES, WHO WILL SHE STAY WITH?

Finally, as for those women who are widowed and then marry again, the following is relevant. Umm Habībah ◈, the wife of the Prophet ﷺ, said:

"O Messenger of Allāh ﷺ, if a woman had two husbands in this life, then they all died and came together in Paradise, with which of them would she be – the first or the last?" He ﷺ said: "With the one whose attitude and conduct with her was best. O Umm Habībah, a good attitude brings one the best of this world and the Hereafter". [175]

May Allāh ﷻ make the events of 'Yawmideen' easy for us, may Allāh ﷻ admit us into Paradise with ease. Āmīn

VERSE 4

﴾٤﴿ إِيَّاكَ نَعْبُدُ وَإِيَّاكَ نَسْتَعِينُ

You alone do we worship, and from You alone do we seek help.

In the opening three verses, Allāh ﷻ utilises His own glorious name and magnificent attributes of Godhood, of sustaining and nurturing the entire creation, of His intensive and extensive mercy, and of His absolute power to

---

[174] Bayhaqi, Tabari, Abu Yala, Fathu'l-Baari, Tabrānī.
[175] al-Tadhkirah fī Aḥwāl al-Mawtá wa-Umūr al-Ākhirah, 2:278.

call to account: Praise belongs to Allāh ﷻ, the Rabb of all the created entities, the very merciful, the owner of the Day of Judgement.

ELOQUENCE IN ADDRESSING THE ALMIGHTY

Following this, in the fourth verse, there is an unexpected turn to first-person expressions with usage of the word 'You', and suddenly we are now in conversation with the Almighty Allāh ﷻ Himself. This eloquent and unusual style of changing expressions is used to generate recognition of Allāh ﷻ and familiarity.

An acquaintance of mine visited me with an associate of his, and whilst introducing him he happened to also mention the name of the village he was from, which happened to be a well-known place to me. As a result of this connection, a sense of recognition and familiarity was generated. I then began conversing with this previously unknown person directly in first-person terms, and vice versa.

Similarly, in the opening verses of Sūrah Fātiha, first-person usage and direct conversation with Allāh ﷻ comes into being once recognition is established with regards to Whom we are conversing with; none but the Almighty Allāh ﷻ. Once this is established, we then acknowledge our worship is for Allāh ﷻ alone, who, being the Supreme Rabb of all created entities, the all-Merciful and the Master of the Day of Judgement, is the only one deserving of worship.

The exclusivity of worship for Allāh ﷻ is expressed in the words [إِيَّاكَ نَعْبُدُ], literally 'You alone.' In *Talkhīsul Miftāh*, the work on Arabic eloquence, this style is explained thus:

'The wording ought to be, نعبدك ونستعينك 'We worship You and we seek help from You' but by bringing in the 'kāf' to begin the sentence, إِيَّاكَ نَعْبُدُ وَإِيَّاكَ نَسْتَعِينُ exclusivity of worship for Allāh alone is established.'

THE REALITY OF WORSHIP

What is worship? Qāḍhī Baidhāwī ☆ writes:

العبادة أقصى غاية الخضوع والتذلل

*'Devotion, humility, and submission of the
absolute highest accord, defines "worship.'*

From all the creations of Allāh ﷻ, humankind has been created as the most honoured and dignified, and the forehead and what it symbolises manifests this honour and dignity. To place this most honourable part of the body on the ground in submission is the pinnacle of obedience and compliance, and there cannot be a greater manifestation of obedience and compliance than by doing so.

Submission can be expressed in various ways and to various extents. One such way is to bow slightly when greeting someone, as is customary in certain communities. A man bowed slightly when greeting the great Muhaddith, Shaykh Yūnus Ḥāfizahullāh, who immediately rebuked him, 'Bowing is only before Allāh ﷻ.' Placing one's hands together and bowing as a mark of respect is also a custom found in some communities. This is sometimes the case in martial arts.

Other forms of expressing submission, devotion, and humility are remaining hungry through fasting, spending money for good causes through zakāh and sadaqah, and performing the annual pilgrimage and its rituals. These forms of worship and everything else which constitutes 'worship' must always be for Allāh ﷻ, and for Him alone.

BOWING IN KARATE

A friend of mine who was very talented in Karate once said to me, 'An integral part of the art is bowing down before bouts, and I have been told I cannot

117

attain the highest grade of Karate, the black belt, without bowing before the masters of this art. I explained the concept of monotheism and of not bowing to anyone besides Allāh ﷻ to my Karate teacher who accepted and understood my position, and he continued teaching me. When it came to the final round and earning the black belt, he said to me, "You will not have any choice besides bowing in the final, you will be before the masters of this art and they will not accept any less."'

My friend replied, 'I will not bow down, even if it means losing out on the black belt.' He wanted to learn the skill which he did, but he did not compromise on his deen for the black belt. Nonetheless, had he bowed down, he would not have become a polytheist and he would not have left the fold of Islam. He would have remained a Muslim, at most, it would be a sin.

TWO CATEGORIES OF PROSTRATION

To bow down or prostrate before someone/something falls into two categories:
1. Prostration of worship.
2. Prostration of respect.

A prostration of worship before something that is normally worshipped is polytheism, and there is no exception to this. To prostrate before idols, for example, is an instance of this, as these are objects which are worshipped.

If one prostrates in front of someone or something which is not an object of worship, then the intention will be taken into account.

If the intention behind the prostration was worship, then this will also be seen as an act of polytheism. If the intention is not so, but rather the intention behind the prostration is to honour and respect, then this will not constitute polytheism but would still be Harām, forbidden and a major sin. Instances of this could be to prostrate before a king, queen, president, teacher, etc.

PROSTRATING OUT OF RESPECT FOR SOMEONE IS HARĀM IN OUR SHARĪ'AH

The prohibition of the prostration of respect has been forbidden in the teachings of the Prophet Mohammed ﷺ, and was not forbidden in the laws of the previous Prophets ﷺ. The prostration of the angels before Adam ﷺ was a prostration of respect and honour, and was not a prostration of worship.

The family of Yūsuf ﷺ prostrating before him, when reunited in Egypt after many long years of separation, was a prostration of honour and respect. As the Prophet Yūsuf ﷺ, the king, was seating his respected father, Prophet Yaqūb ﷺ, on his throne, his brothers and the rest of the family fell into prostrations of honour and respect. This was the manifestation of the dream Yūsuf ﷺ had seen in his childhood, when he dreamt of the sun, the moon, and eleven stars prostrating before him.

THE HADĪTH ON REQUESTING TO PROSTRATE BEFORE THE PROPHET ﷺ

The Prophet ﷺ once sent an expedition to the Roman Empire. Upon their return, a companion by the name of Qais bin Saad bin Ubādah ﷺ requested permission from the Prophet ﷺ to prostrate before him, as they had seen the citizens of the Roman Empire do so before their generals. The rationale behind this request was that if they prostrate before their leaders and seniors, then the Prophet of Allāh ﷺ, the most elevated and beloved creation of Allāh ﷻ, is most deserving of this honour, on account of being the ultimate messenger of Allāh ﷻ. The Prophet ﷺ did not agree to this request and instead replied, 'Worship your Rabb and honour your brother.' [176]

The Prophet ﷺ considered himself to be a human being as well, and this fact is established from the Qur'ān and Hadīth, and although he is the chosen

---

[176] Mishkāt.

one of Allāh 🜲, he should be treated as a human, a created being, and not equal with the rank of Allāh 🜲, the Creator.

The Prophet 🜲 said that if it were right for one human to prostrate to another, he would have commanded women to prostrate to their husbands because of the greater rights that they have over them. [177]

If the Prophet 🜲 had given this command, our mothers and sisters would now be in a dilemma, for they would have to prostrate before their husbands every day. When they find it difficult to prostrate before Allāh 🜲 in salāh, how would they have prostrated before their husbands?

This statement of considering the command of prostration before the husband was made by the Prophet 🜲 to drive home the status and rank of the husband before the wife. Otherwise, prostration is for Allāh 🜲 alone, and the laws of shari'ah prohibits the prostration of respect for any created being and only allows the prostration for worship of Allāh 🜲.

SAJDAH OF SHUKR

The prostration of gratitude [Sajdah-e-Shukr] before Allāh 🜲 is desirable and recommended. Some Muslim sportsmen fall into prostration upon accomplishing a hard task, e.g scoring a goal, or scoring one hundred [100] runs. They do this to show gratitude. The prostration of gratitude can be performed for Allāh 🜲 only. This type of prostration is considered to be makrooh in the Hanafī School of Thought, although there is one opinion of the famous student of Imām Abu Hanīfah 🜲, Imām Muhammad 🜲, that this prostration is sunnah in agreement with the other two Schools of Thought [Shafi'i, and Hanbalī] that recognise this prostration, and opine that this is one prostration of appreciation established from some narrations, just as the prostrations of recital [Sajdah-e-Tilāwah] are recognised and applicable on reciting or hearing particular verses.

---

[177] Mishkāt.

120

At the conclusion of the battle of Badr, the Prophet ﷺ sent a few individuals to search for and determine the fate of Abu Jahl. Abdullāh bin Mas'ūd ؓ returned and informed the Prophet ﷺ of the demise of Abu Jahl. The Prophet ﷺ fell into prostration, and expressed relief at the death of such an oppressive individual. This prostration was for Allāh ﷻ alone and the Prophet ﷺ did perform such a sajdāh on this occasion.

Some people take sajdāh-e-shukr as a regular sunnah. They even say that wudhū is not necessary and you don't need to face the Qiblah either. This is totally baseless. Both are necessary, as sajdah is like salāh and will require all its pre-requisites of covering the satr, and also the clothes, body and place of worship being clean etc.

There were many occasions of happiness during the life of the Prophet ﷺ, but we do not find him doing sajdah of shukr all the time, therefore, it cannot be classed as a continuous sunnah.

Īmām Abu Hanifa and Īmām Maalik ؓ are of the opinion that a person should pray two rak'at salaah for shukr. This is a complete way of worship. They also say that Allāh's ﷻ blessings are plenty, so we can't keep doing sajdāh for every blessing. May Allāh ﷻ give us the ability to be grateful to Him for all His bounties, and to appreciate His favours from the depths of our hearts. Āmīn!

WORSHIP AND ITS PURPOSE

This is the essence of 'You alone we worship.' Allāh ﷻ, in a number of places in the Qur'ān, commands fulfilment of this action of worshipping Him:

$$وَلِلَّهِ غَيْبُ السَّمَاوَاتِ وَالْأَرْضِ$$

$$وَإِلَيْهِ يُرْجَعُ الْأَمْرُ كُلُّهُ فَاعْبُدْهُ وَتَوَكَّلْ عَلَيْهِ ۞$$

To Allāh belongs the unseen things of the heavens and the earth and to

121

Him Alone will all matters return. <u>So worship Him</u> and rely on Him only. [178]

And:

يَا أَيُّهَا النَّاسُ اعْبُدُوا رَبَّكُمُ الَّذِي خَلَقَكُمْ وَالَّذِينَ مِن قَبْلِكُمْ لَعَلَّكُمْ تَتَّقُونَ ❂

O people! Worship your Rabb Who created you and Who created those before you, so that you may develop Taqwā [piety]. [179]

The purpose of worship is to cultivate God-consciousness in the heart, and worship in its various forms will breed and increase this wonderful quality within us, ultimately leading us to the achievement of our objective of living wholesome and pure God-conscious lives. For instance, fasting develops God-consciousness and Zakāh cleans the heart of greed and of the love for worldly pleasures.

Allāh ﷻ gives this command of worship in numerous places in the Qur'ān:

يَا أَيُّهَا الَّذِينَ آمَنُوا ارْكَعُوا وَاسْجُدُوا

وَاعْبُدُوا رَبَّكُمْ وَافْعَلُوا الْخَيْرَ لَعَلَّكُمْ تُفْلِحُونَ ❂

O you who have Imaan, bow down, prostrate, worship your Rabb and carry out good deeds so that you may be successful. [180]

And:

وَمِنْ آيَاتِهِ اللَّيْلُ وَالنَّهَارُ وَالشَّمْسُ وَالْقَمَرُ ۚ لَا تَسْجُدُوا لِلشَّمْسِ

---

[178] Qur'ān 11:123.

[179] Qur'ān 2:21.

[180] Qur'ān 22:77, Upon reciting this verse, followers of the Imām Shāfi'ī and Hanbalī Fiqh <u>only</u> should perform Sajdāh-e-Tilāwah. [Qur'ān made Easy, pg.597].

$$\text{وَلَا لِلْقَمَرِ وَاسْجُدُوا لِلَّهِ الَّذِي خَلَقَهُنَّ إِن كُنتُمْ إِيَّاهُ تَعْبُدُونَ ۩}$$

From among Allāh's Aayaat are the night, the day, the sun, and the moon. Do not prostrate to the sun, nor to the moon, but prostrate to Allāh Who created them, if you are to worship Him alone. [181]

WORSHIP SHOULD BE FOR ALLĀH ﷻ ALONE

Today the rationale of humankind has become redundant. Two thirds do not believe in this beautiful message of Allāh ﷻ and His Qur'ān. They prostrate to idols. A great number of them are expert academics, professionals, and intellectuals in a range of subjects related to the life of this world, such as doctors, lawyers, scientists, and professors. With such expertise and intellect, what brings these people to bow down before idols, an action that leaves us to wonder – where has the application of this 'expert intelligence and understanding' gone?

Do these so-called experts not have that level of understanding to know that idols are not deities from which expectations of any kind can be met? These are merely man-made decorated statues and nothing more. They cannot be of any help or benefit whatsoever. Worship is the command of the one true God, Allāh ﷻ, and is for Him alone. Allāh ﷻ detests all associations of partners with Him in any way, shape or form. The Qur'ān says:

$$\text{إِنَّ اللَّهَ لَا يَغْفِرُ أَن يُشْرَكَ بِهِ وَيَغْفِرُ مَا دُونَ ذَٰلِكَ لِمَن يَشَاءُ}$$

$$\text{وَمَن يُشْرِكْ بِاللَّهِ فَقَدْ ضَلَّ ضَلَالًا بَعِيدًا ۩}$$

Verily Allāh shall not forgive that Shirk be committed but will forgive all other

---

[181] Qur'ān 41:37, Upon reciting this verse, Sajdāh-e-Tilāwah should be made.

sins for whom He wills. Whoever ascribes partners to Allāh has strayed far away.
182

POLYTHEISM POLLUTES GOOD DEEDS

If a bottle of the finest beverage is before you and a drop of filth was thrown into the bottle, what would be left of the drink? Similarly, carrying out an act of great good, but contaminating it with polytheistic beliefs renders the act itself impure, and is therefore not accepted in the court of Allāh ﷻ. You must only bring to the court of Allāh ﷻ actions that are free and clean from the filth of polytheism, only then can there be hope for acceptance. The soul and spirit of our actions is created by faith.

SHIRK IS LIFELESS! ĪMĀN BREATHES LIFE

Riding a horse will take you from one place to another in very little time, whilst sitting on a wooden horse will take you nowhere. The wooden horse is lifeless and has no soul, whereas the living horse has both. Similarly, the life and spirit of our actions will be created by true faith alone, and actions of true faith will then reach the court of Allāh ﷻ.

This is the lesson being ingrained into us in this verse as we repeat this exclusivity of worship to Allāh ﷻ alone constantly throughout the day.

A GOOD QUESTION

One Sahābi ؓ came to the Prophet ﷺ and asked, 'O Rasūlullāh ﷺ, please advise me of the actions that will bring me closer to Paradise and take me

---

182 Qur'ān 4:116.

further away from the Fire of Hell.' The Prophet ﷺ liked the question and admired the Sahābi ﷺ. [183]

When I myself go to any programme, I do not take any Q&A sessions as the only questions people are interested in asking are on insurance, mortgages, divorce and the like, and no other issues come to the attention of people, so why should I get involved in this kind of questioning? It is better to engage in worship than to entertain such questions. People have lost the understanding of what good questioning is, whereas the Sahābā ﷺ asked such poignant and useful questions.

The Prophet ﷺ admired the question and replied:

تعبد الله ولا تشرك به شيأ وتقيم الصلوة المكتوبة

وتؤدي الزكوة المفروضة وتصل الرحم

'Worship Allāh, and do not ascribe partners with Allāh,
keep steadfast on Salāh, give Zakāh, and join ties." [184]

Hajj was not included in the answer of the Prophet ﷺ, possibly because Hajj was not made obligatory at that time, or because Hajj is a once in a lifetime obligation, and on individuals who are financially and physically able to perform it. Nonetheless, the important worships of salāh and zakāh were included in this answer of the Prophet ﷺ to drive home their importance and significance. Furthermore, particular mention was made of maintaining family ties, because the questioner was a Bedouin from the villages, whose disposition could be abrupt and sometimes rude. So the Prophet ﷺ advised him to adopt softness and kindness in his dealings with those around him. These are the forms of worship, salāh and zakāh, which will draw you closer to Heaven and distance you from Hell.

---

[183] Muslim, Mishkāt.
[184] Muslim.

May Allāh ﷻ grant us the capability to fully accomplish all types of worship. Āmīn!

WORSHIP IS FOR LIFE

Be very particular about fulfilling your Islamic obligations. Do not settle on being a seasonal 'Ramadhān Muslim', rather become a complete life-long Muslim. Some people behave as Muslims in Ramadhān only, and once Ramadhān is over they revert to their old ways until the following Ramadhān arrives. Similarly, some Huffāz only revise the Qur'ān in Ramadhān to lead the Tarāwīh, and once this is done the Qur'ān is left unopened until the following Ramadhān arrives. As a result of this eleven month neglect, panic begins to set in at having to revise and lead Tarāwīh. If the Qur'ān was recited throughout the year, there would be no need to panic and the Qur'ān would be well-maintained for Tarāwīh too. Fulfilling your obligations throughout the year rather than seasonally, will draw you closer to Heaven and distance you from Hell.

Some women spend their Ramadhān in pious worship and, once Ramadhān is over, the prayer mat and Tasbīh are tucked away until next year. How will blessings and goodness enter such a home, and how will the children then live an Islamic lifestyle if this is the condition of the home? If the child sees the zeal of salāh in the parent, then the same will be developed in the child. The first step on the ladder of worship is the performance and establishment of salāh, from which other acts of obedience and restraint from disobedience will follow. May Allāh ﷻ give us the tawfīq. Āmīn

SEEKING HELP FROM ALLĀH ALONE ﷻ

We will now move into the second part of the verse: وَإِيَّاكَ نَسْتَعِينُ 'From You alone do we seek assistance.'

If we need support of any kind, help with issues with family life, medical conditions, employment, or any other kind of problem, we should seek help from Allāh 🕮, as Allāh 🕮 is the only one who has the power to remove these problems.

Allāh 🕮 gives such commands of relying upon Him in numerous places in the Qur'ān:

$$\text{فَاعْبُدْهُ وَتَوَكَّلْ عَلَيْهِ ۝}$$

So Worship [only] Him and rely on Him only. [185]

And:

$$\text{وَمَن يَتَوَكَّلْ عَلَى اللَّهِ فَهُوَ حَسْبُهُ ۝}$$

Allāh is sufficient for the one who trusts in Him. [186]

Turn only to Allāh 🕮 when seeking help, and have trust in Him alone, and He will come to your aid.

And:

$$\text{وَعَلَى اللَّهِ فَلْيَتَوَكَّلِ الْمُؤْمِنُونَ ۝}$$

Only in Allāh should the believers trust. [187]

TURNING TO JINN AND JĀDŪ

At times Shaytān will launch extremely sophisticated and cunning attacks on an unsuspecting person, leading them to chase every other person for help, rather than turning to Allāh 🕮. Sometimes this is done through those who dress in the guise of religion, masquerading as men of God, there to solve every

---

[185] Qur'ān 11:123.

[186] Qur'ān 65:3.

[187] Qur'ān 64:13.

problem a person may be facing. They always scare people with Jinn and Jādū [sorcery]. Then they claim to cure such people.

Only Allāh ﷻ can remove real difficulties. No one else can do so, especially not the one who has no internal piety.

SUPPORTING THE DEEN

If you assist the religion of Allāh ﷻ and give your service to it, then Allāh ﷻ will surely repay you many times more with His divine assistance and favours. This can be done by simply sitting with the people of Allāh ﷻ, i.e the pious, by spending time in the path of Allāh ﷻ, and by making the time and effort to properly learn the religion of Allāh ﷻ. This is the assistance of the religion of Allāh ﷻ, as is propagating it in its true form, whether it is done at your work place, home, or community.

If you do the work of Allāh ﷻ, Allāh ﷻ will aid you in doing your own, and this is the message of the second part of this verse.

SEEKING HELP IN WORLDLY MATTERS

To seek help in worldly matters and utilising the means at your disposal is permitted. For example if I am thirsty and I request someone to bring me a glass of water, I am seeking the assistance of another human but this would not constitute polytheism. It's normal for a human to ask another for help. This level of seeking help has been recorded from the practice of the Prophet ﷺ, who once, upon proceeding to answer the call of nature, told Abdullāh bin Mas'ūd ؓ to search for and bring three stones. He was unable to find three stones, but found two stones and some dried manure which he brought back with him. The Prophet ﷺ took the two stones but threw the manure away and commented, 'This is impurity'. He then used the two stones to complete the call of nature. [188]

---

[188] Bukhārī: 156.

The Prophet ﷺ would tell Anas ﷺ, his attendant, to do certain tasks of calling a particular person or other similar menial tasks. One person cannot do everything himself/herself, and is in need of help at times to fulfil tasks.

THREE TYPES OF HELP DURING WUDHŪ

There is an issue of discussion in this regard in the books of Fiqh, related to wudhū and taking assistance from others in performing wudhū. There are three stages of taking assistance when doing wudhū:

1. Asking someone to fill the jug and keep it ready for wudhū. This level of assistance is permitted.

2. Requesting the person who brought the jug to pour the water onto your limbs and you do wudhū yourself whilst he/she pours the water. This is permitted at times of necessity.

3. To have someone else wash your limbs for you. This is only permitted when a person is incapable of doing wudhū themselves, for reasons of illness for example. This method is not permitted without dire necessity.

SEEKING HELP IN MATTERS BEYOND HUMAN CAPACITY

To seek help in matters which are over and above our capabilities, and not related to using the means at our disposal, is for Allāh ﷻ alone. For example, a couple without children, an individual without employment or without money, or a person facing a severe problem or difficulty of some sort, only Allāh ﷻ alone has the capability to assist and help in overcoming these issues. We will not turn to people to give us children or sustenance, for this is the dominion of Allāh ﷻ alone.

The polytheists of Makkah would do this. They kept three hundred and sixty [360] idols by the Ka'ba and each idol was designated to fulfil certain needs, such as the idol for giving children, the idol for distributing sustenance, etc. The polytheists would turn to the appropriate idol depending on their needs. This level of seeking assistance is exclusive for Allāh ﷻ alone, because only Allāh ﷻ can come to our aid in these situations.

ASKING SOMEONE TO PRAY FOR YOU

To request someone else to pray to Allāh on your behalf is permitted, particularly the pious friends of Allāh ﷻ. If you were to request such people of piety to pray for you for ease in overcoming these kinds of issues, then it is possible, that due to their strong connection and relationship with Allāh ﷻ, Allāh ﷻ will look favourably upon their duās.

If you open books of Hadīth, you will find many examples where the Sahābā requested the Prophet ﷺ to make Dua for them. Umme Sulaym ؓ said: "Ya Rasūlallāh! Pray for your khādim Anas." He ﷺ lifted his hands and said:

اللهم اكثر ماله وولده وبارك له فى عمره واغفر له

"O Allāh! Increase his wealth and children, bless him in his lifespan, and forgive him."

Anas ؓ lived for over a hundred years, had plenty of children and owned many properties. He said I am hoping for forgiveness. [189]

One Sahābī requested for Dua that rain falls as there was a severe drought. The Prophet ﷺ lifted his hands, made Dua, and the clouds appeared immediately, it then began to rain heavily. [190]

Abu Huraira ؓ said: "Ya Rasūlallāh! Make Dua that Allāh gives guidance to my mother." He did so and Abu Huraira ؓ returned home happily. His mother was having a shower and immediately afterwards, she declared the Sahādah. [191] The list goes on.

---

[189] Al-Adab Al-Mufrad.

[190] Bukhārī.

[191] Mishkāt.

ASKING THE DEAD FOR HELP

Another issue arises with regards to visiting the graves of the pious and beseeching the individual in the grave to assist in fulfilling some need, such as removing sickness, granting children etc. This is totally unacceptable and not permitted, for only Allāh ﷻ can do these things and only Allāh ﷻ can be asked in such a manner.

Once I overheard a Hājī sahib in Makkah Mukarramah who had come to perform Hajj. He must have had a habit of visiting the grave of Hadhrat Daata Sahib in Lahore. Whilst in Hajj, he fell ill and in his ignorance, he phoned his family in Lahore, requesting them to go to the grave of Hadhrat Daata sahib in Lahore and beseech him for shifa. Instead of going to the Kaa'ba shareef and turning to Allāh ﷻ in the holiest of lands, he turned to the individual in the grave. Such behaviour can not only lead to polytheism, but is a polytheistic action in itself. When this kind of mind-set is created in an individual, correct understanding and judgement becomes clouded.

Sufi Abdul Hamīd Sawāti ﷵ writes, 'Once, in the month of Rajab, I mounted a horse cart in which another person was seated with his fit and healthy goat. We began to engage in conversation and I praised the goat, to which he replied, "Yes, I am taking it for Qurbāni [ritual slaughter]."

'I was confused. "This is the month of Rajab, and Qurbāni is in Dhul-Hijjah, which is yet five months away. Which Qurbāni are you doing?" He replied, "The Qurbāni at the grave of Hadhrat Daata Saheb."[192] I explained, "Qurbāni is in Dhul-Hijjah, in the name of Allāh ﷻ and for the sake of Allāh ﷻ alone, this Qurbāni at the grave of Hadhrat Daata Saheb in Rajab is nothing." The man refused to listen and was adamant he would slaughter the goat there and distribute the meat among the locals.'

Qurbāni is an act of worship, and worship is the exclusive area of Allāh ﷻ alone; this is what Allāh ﷻ is imparting in this verse of Sūrah Fātiha.

---

[192] Sayyed Ali Hajweri ﷵ.

WASEELAH AND TAWASSUL

In relation to the issue of seeking assistance, the matter of *Tawassul* arises, which is asking Allāh ﷻ to fulfil some need through the means of a pious deed or pious personality.

This is permitted and there is a plethora of authentic evidence to strongly support this position. Sometimes, the Prophet ﷺ would do this, as reported the Hadīth of *Mishkāt*:

كان رسول الله صلى الله عليه وسلم يستفتح بصعاليك المهاجرين

Rasulullah ﷺ *would beg for victory through the poor among the migrants.* [193] [194]

To make duā to Allāh ﷻ and hoping for acceptance through the blessings of the Holy Book of Allāh ﷻ is a similarly accepted means of *Tawassul*. One of the loftiest methods of this is through the means of the Prophet ﷺ himself. We are still asking Allāh ﷻ, but through the means of something/someone closely connected to Allāh ﷻ, so that through this close connection Allāh ﷻ will also look upon our duā favourably.

In Sahih Bukhārī, the poetry of Abu Tālib is narrated:

وأبيض يستسقى الغمام بوجهه ثمال اليتامى عصمة للأرامل

The fair complex young man through whose face rain is sought from
the clouds. The refuge of orphans and the protections for the widows. [195]

The Prophet ﷺ did not object to the couplet which is an approval from his side.

---

[193] Mishkāt Munziri Haythami.

[194] 4/142 رواه المنذري في الترغيب والترهب

وقال رواته رواة الصحيح وهو مرسل والهيثمى في مجمع الزوائد وقال رجاله رجال الصحيح 10/265

[195] Bukhārī: 1009.

During the time of Umar ﷜ a drought struck Madinah Shareef. He went to the outskirts and supplicated for rain. Abbas ibn Abdul Muttalib was with him. He said:

اللهم أناكنا نتوسل اليك بنبيك صلى الله عليه وسلم

فتسقينا ، وانا نتوسل اليك بعم نبيك فاسقنا

Ya Allāh! We used to beseech you through your Prophet and You used to give us rain. We now beg you through your prophet's uncle so give us rain. Allāh sent the clouds and it began to rain. [196]

On another occasion, Bilal ibn Harith Al-Muzani came to the grave of the Prophet ﷺ and requested for Duās for rain. He said:

يا رسول الله استسق الله لأمتك فانهم قد هلكوا

Ya Rasūlallāh! Pray for rain for your Ummah, because they have been destroyed.

He saw Rasūlullāh ﷺ in a dream, who said: "Go to Umar! Give him my salams and tell him you will be assisted with rain. However, hold onto intelligence. Be intelligent." He came to Umar and informed him. Umar began to cry and said: My Rabb! I will not fall short as long as I am able to do so." [197]

These incidents demonstrate the beliefs the companions ﷠ held with regards to the issue of *Tawassul* and seeking the acceptance of duās through the means of the Prophet ﷺ.

To seek assistance through the means of the Prophet ﷺ is perfectly acceptable. If, in Madinah Munawwarah, you should stand before the blessed resting place of the Prophet ﷺ, present your greetings to the great master ﷺ and then request him to seek forgiveness for you. This is indeed a noble and accepted deed. To request the Prophet ﷺ himself to forgive your sins is

---

[196] Bukhārī 3710.

[197] Musnad Al-Farooq 1/23. Ibn Kathīr said: اسناد جيد قوى

wrong, because the Prophet ﷺ is not the forgiver of sins. It is Allāh ﷻ alone who forgives sins. We should ask Allāh ﷻ for forgiveness or ask the Prophet ﷺ to intercede for us.

To label such requests as polytheism is wholly incorrect and a misunderstanding of what *Tawassul* is.

The Bedouin, Atabi, came by the resting place of the Prophet ﷺ just three days after his passing, offered salām before him, and then said, 'How wonderful it was whilst you were alive; if we had slipped up or erred then you would raise your hands and seek forgiveness for us from Allāh ﷻ, and we would be forgiven. But now that you are no more with us, where can we go and who can we turn to, to seek forgiveness for us? Our recourse is to recite this verse only . . .'

وَلَوْ أَنَّهُمْ إِذْ ظَلَمُوا أَنْفُسَهُمْ جَاءُوكَ فَاسْتَغْفَرُوا اللَّهَ

وَاسْتَغْفَرَ لَهُمُ الرَّسُولُ لَوَجَدُوا اللَّهَ تَوَّابًا رَحِيمًا ۞

If only it were that when they wrong themselves, they would come to you seeking Allāh's forgiveness; and then the Rasul seeks forgiveness on their behalf, they will then surely find that Allāh is Most Forgiving, Most Merciful. [198]

He then began weeping and turned to leave. As he walked away, a voice from the unseen was heard saying, 'Tell Atabi, I sought forgiveness on his behalf and he has been forgiven.' [199]

Hence, this practice has been established from the era of the companions ﷺ and only in recent times have people begun to question it and raised flawed objections against it. These people claim to follow the practices of the pious

---

[198] Qur'ān 4:64.

[199] Fadhail-e-Durood Shareef.

predecessors [The *Salaf*], so is this not the practice of the early pious predecessors?

Sufi Abdul Hamīd Sawāti would say, 'Some people say:

يا شيخ عبد القادر شيأ لله

"O Shaikh, Master Abdul Qādir Jīlāni! Give us something for the sake of Allāh!"

But he is buried in Baghdad and we are sitting here on the other side of the world, so how is he to hear what we are saying?'

This is the inappropriate method. However, if one was to say:

يا الله شيأ للشيخ عبد القادر

*'O Allāh , for the sake of Shaikh Abdul Qādir's relationship
and spiritual proximity to you, grant us this bounty'.*

This would be correct, for we are beseeching the assistance and aid of Allāh only, but through the means of a pious personality.

So وَإِيَّاكَ نَسْتَعِينُ means seeking Allāh's help only in all our affairs. This should reach the highest level of tawakkul.

We have an article on www.tafseer-reheemi.com with regards to Tawassul. Please refer to it for more information.

VERSE 5

﴾ ٥ ﴿ اهْدِنَا الصِّرَاطَ الْمُسْتَقِيمَ

Show us the straight path.

The phrase [اِهْدِنَا] is from the root word 'hidāyah', meaning 'guidance' or more specifically 'spiritual guidance'. Variations of the word 'hidāyah' appear in many places in the Qur'ān:

إِنَّكَ لَا تَهْدِي مَنْ أَحْبَبْتَ وَلَٰكِنَّ اللَّهَ

135

$$\text{يَهْدِي مَن يَشَاءُ ۚ وَهُوَ أَعْلَمُ بِالْمُهْتَدِينَ ۞}$$

You cannot give guidance to whomsoever you wish, but Allāh gives guidance to whomsoever He wills, and He best knows the ones who are rightly guided. [200]

And:

$$\text{قُلْ هَلْ مِن شُرَكَائِكُم مَّن يَهْدِي إِلَى الْحَقِّ ۚ قُلِ اللَّهُ يَهْدِي لِلْحَقِّ ۗ أَفَمَن يَهْدِي}$$

$$\text{إِلَى الْحَقِّ أَحَقُّ أَن يُتَّبَعَ أَمَّن لَّا يَهِدِّي إِلَّا أَن يُهْدَىٰ ۖ فَمَا لَكُمْ كَيْفَ تَحْكُمُونَ ۞}$$

Say, "Is there any one from your associate-gods who guides to the truth?" Say, "Allāh guides to the truth. Is, then, He who guides to the truth more worthy of being obeyed, or he who has no guidance at all unless he is guided [i.e carried by someone else]? So, what has happened to you? How do you judge things? [201]

The word also appears in ahādīth. 'Ali ﷺ reported that Allāh's Messenger ﷺ said to him:

$$\text{قُلِ اللَّهُمَّ اهْدِنِي وَسَدِّدْنِي وَاذْكُرْ بِالْهُدَى}$$

$$\text{هِدَايَتَكَ الطَّرِيقَ وَالسَّدَادِ سَدَادَ السَّهْمِ}$$

Say, 'O Allāh, guide me upon the right path and keep me straight,' and [when you make a mention of right guidance] think of yourself travelling on the correct road which leads you to your destination, and by keeping straight [sadād] think of the setting right [or straightness] of an arrow. [202]

The purpose of this prayer is to ask to be spiritually guided and kept upon the correct path which leads to the desired destination. As Muslims who believe

---

[200] Qur'ān 28:56.

[201] Qur'ān 10:35.

[202] Muslim: 2725 a; Nasa'ī: 5212, 5376; Abu Dāwūd: 4225.

136

in Allāh ﷻ and the Last Day, our desired destination is to please our Rabb and creator, Allāh ﷻ Himself. Allāh ﷻ has created a place in which those who earn his pleasure dwell, and that place is Jannah [Paradise]. Our goal is to reach those gardens through pleasing Him. To do this, we must realise that life itself is the journey, and Allāh's ﷻ chosen faith is the road. If we veer away from the path, if we stray away from Islam's teachings, we will never reach our destination. So we must become punctual in our salāh, punctual in our fasts, and punctual in our zakāh. We must make the Hajj pilgrimage, and we must attempt to stay away from all sins and innovations. We must reject participation in all innovative customs which take place at times of happiness [weddings, Eid, etc.] or times of sorrow [funerals, etc.]. And when we stray, we must repent and seek forgiveness immediately, and return to the path. This is why the prophet of Allāh ﷺ tells us to ask Allāh ﷻ to keep us on the straight path, and to help us adhere to it and move along it as swift and as direct as a loosed arrow towards its target.

As for the exits that lead off this path to our destination, they are the undesirable acts, the disliked acts, and the major and minor sins. The more and more we commit these and commit to these actions, the farther and farther away from the straight path will we stray. Until, Allāh ﷻ forbid, one comes upon the road to *Kufr* and disbelief. Then to return to the straight path becomes nigh on impossible, as all the twists and turns and exits have left it far, far behind and out of sight. So when we stray a little from the path, we must repent and seek forgiveness immediately, and return to it. To err is human, yet if we remain close to the path, we can always return. However, if we do not turn back to it, and stray too far, the path will be lost to us. This is why Abu Sa'id al-Khudri ﷺ states that Allāh's Messenger ﷺ said:

مَثَلُ الْمُؤْمِنِ وَمَثَلُ الْإِيمَانِ كَمَثَلِ الْفَرَسِ فِي آخِيَّتِهِ يَجُولُ ثُمَّ يَرْجِعُ إِلَى آخِيَّتِهِ وَإِنَّ الْمُؤْمِنَ يَسْهُو ثُمَّ يَرْجِعُ إِلَى الْإِيمَانِ فَأَطْعِمُوا طَعَامَكُمُ الْأَتْقِيَاءَ وَأَوْلُوا مَعْرُوفَكُمُ الْمُؤْمِنِينَ

137

The example of the believer with regards to [his/her] faith is like the example of a horse with regards to its tethering stake; it roams around and then returns to its tethering stake, and the believer does forget and then he/she returns to his/her faith. So feed the pious with your food and show your kindness to the [complete] believers.' [203]

The tethering stake is a person's Īmān, to which he is tied. Even when a Mu'min makes a mistake, or strays, as he/she is tethered to it, he/she will always return back to it. However, if the person pulls too hard upon the rope, the stake will be uprooted and he/she will lose their connection to Īmān. So we must stay close to it and never wander too far. Because of the real and present danger of this, the beloved Prophet ﷺ advised us to do two things in order to protect our Īmān:

$$ فَأَطْعِمُوا طَعَامَكُمُ الْأَتْقِيَاءَ وَأَوْلُوا مَعْرُوفَكُمُ الْمُؤْمِنِينَ $$

He ﷺ advises us firstly to 'feed the pious' with our food and secondly to 'treat the believers well'. Feeding the pious and inviting them to your house encourages their duās [prayers] for you and your family. It also brings the blessings that constantly shower upon such people, into your homes. Also, it provides an opportunity for you to receive advice and spiritual guidance from them, and acquaints your children with the company and influence of the pious. As for treating the believers well, it means to greet them kindly and give gifts to them. Salām is a form of duā which encourages the recipient to reply 'wa-'alaikum-salām' and make duā for you in return. The giving of gifts to believers softens their hearts towards you and encourages them to reply with 'jazāk-Allāh', another form of duā for you. Through this we learn that the company of the pious and the prayers and goodwill of the believers are a sure means of protecting our Īmān.

---

[203] Ahmad: 11132.

There are also other actions mentioned in aḥādīth to help in protecting our Īmān. In one hadīth, 'Abdullah bin 'Amr ﷺ states that the Messenger of Allāh ﷺ said:

$$اسْتَقِيمُوا وَلَنْ تُحْصُوا وَاعْلَمُوا أَنَّ خَيْرَ أَعْمَالِكُمُ الصَّلَاةُ وَلَا يُحَافِظُ عَلَى الْوُضُوءِ إِلَّا مُؤْمِنٌ$$

Adhere to righteousness even though you will not be able to do all acts of virtue. Know that among the best of your deeds is prayer [salāh] and that no one safeguards wudhū [by staying in the state of wudhū at all times] except a believer. [204]

Another hadīth is related by Abu Huraira ﷺ, in which he reports that Allāh's Messenger ﷺ stated:

$$لَنْ يُنَجِّيَ أَحَدًا مِنْكُمْ عَمَلُهُ . قَالُوا وَلَا أَنْتَ يَا رَسُولَ اللَّهِ قَالَ وَلَا أَنَا، إِلَّا أَنْ يَتَغَمَّدَنِي اللَّهُ بِرَحْمَةٍ، سَدِّدُوا وَقَارِبُوا، وَاغْدُوا وَرُوحُوا، وَشَيْءٌ مِنَ الدُّلْجَةِ. وَالْقَصْدَ الْقَصْدَ تَبْلُغُوا$$

'The deeds of anyone of you will not save him [from the hellfire].' They [the Sahābā ﷺ] asked, 'Even you [will not be saved by your deeds], O Allāh's Messenger ﷺ?' He said, 'No, even I, unless Allāh bestows His Mercy on me. Therefore, do good deeds properly, sincerely and moderately, and worship Allāh in the morning and in the evening and during a part of the night, and always adopt a middle, moderate, regular course whereby you will reach your target [Paradise]. [205]

Here, the Holy Prophet ﷺ advises us to make use of certain times of the day to strengthen our connection with Allāh ﷺ and reach our intended goal and

---

[204] Muwatta Mālik: 2/67; Ibn Mājah: 1/290, 291, 292.
[205] Bukhārī: 6463.

destination. As well as this, this hadīth reinforces the fact that hidāyah is in the control of Allāh ﷻ and Allāh ﷻ alone, and only by His divine will do we succeed or fail. No king or priest or saint or prophet can grant a person hidāyah, nor can a person's mere actions free him from the fire. We all need the fadhl of Allāh ﷻ.

Abu Tālib passed away in a state of disbelief [Kufr]. The Holy Prophet ﷺ was much grieved that his beloved uncle who had helped and supported him in every way throughout his life, had died without Īmān. We can only realise just how much love the Holy Prophet ﷺ bore for his uncle, Abu Tālib, through the love and affection he displayed during the funeral and burial of his aunty Fātima Bint Asad ؓ, the wife of Abu Tālib and foster mother of the blessed Prophet ﷺ. Apart from Khadija ؓ, Fātima Bint Asad ؓ was one of the first women to pay allegiance to the Messenger of Allāh ﷺ and enter the fold of Islam, and was well known for her piety and righteousness. [206] As well as this, she also made Hijrah, emigrating from Makkah to Madinah where she passed away.

Regarding her death, Anas bin Malik ؓ narrates that when Fatima bint Asad ؓ, the mother of 'Ali ؓ, passed away, the Messenger of Allāh ﷺ entered her home, sat by her head-side, and said:

رَحِمَكِ اللَّهُ يَا أُمِّي ، كُنْتِ أُمِّي بَعْدَ أُمِّي ، تَجُوعِينَ وَتُشْبِعِينِي ، وَتَعْرَيْنَ وَتَكْسُونَنِي ، وَتَمْنَعِينَ نَفْسَكِ طَيِّبَ الطَّعَامِ وَتُطْعِمِينِي ، تُرِيدِينَ بِذَلِكَ وَجْهَ اللَّهِ وَالدَّارَ الآخِرَةَ

Allāh bless your noble soul, O mother. You were my mother after my mother [passed away]. You fed me while you yourself went hungry. You clothed me while you yourself went without [new] clothes. You prevented yourself from delicious foods and fed me. Your aim in doing so was to attain Allāh's pleasure and the life hereafter.'

---

[206] Muhammad ibn Saad. *Kitāb al-Tabaqāt al-Kabīr* vol. 8. Translated by Bewley, A. (1995). The Women of Madinah, p. 156. London: Ta-Ha Publishers.

After this, he ordered that she be given the ritual bath three times, and when they reached the water perfumed with *Kāfūr* [camphor or eucalyptus] the Messenger of Allāh ﷺ poured it himself. After this, he removed his own sheet [for her burial shroud] and he himself wrapped her in it, and then helped carry her [during the funeral procession to the graveyard]. Then Usāma bin Zayd ﷺ, Abu Ayyūb al-Ansārī ﷺ, Umar bin al-Khattāb ﷺ, and an Abyssinian slave were called to dig the grave which they dug until they reached the *lahad* [internal grave opening]. The Messenger of Allāh ﷺ dug this himself, digging the soil with his blessed hands. Once they had finished, the Messenger of Allāh ﷺ remained in the grave, and then lay down in it and said:

الله الذي يحيي ويميت، وهو حي لا يموت، اغفر لأمي فاطمة بنت أسد، ولقنها

حجتها، ووسع مدخلها بحق نبيك، والأنبياء الذين من قبلي، فإنك أرحم الراحمين

'[O] Allāh, who gives life and causes death, who is and will never die, forgive my mother, Fātima bint Asad, inspire her with her evidence [i.e. answers to Munkar and Nakīr's questions], and grant her expansion in her grave through the advocacy of your Prophet ﷺ and of all the prophets ﷺ before me, for indeed Thou art the Most Merciful of All.' [207]

Then he led her funeral prayer [janāzah] and then she was placed in her grave by the prophet ﷺ himself. The Messenger of Allāh ﷺ was often heard to say, 'I was an orphan and she made me her son. She was the kindest person to me after Abu Tālib.' [208]

Imagine then, if you will, the happiness and joy that Rasūlullah ﷺ would have experienced if his beloved uncle had accepted Islam before his death. Yet it was not decreed to be so. Sa'īd bin al-Musayyib ﷺ reported from his father

---

[207] Tabrānī in *al-Mu'jam al-Kabīr*: 351/24, and *Al-Mu'jam Al-Awsat*: 196; Abu Nu'aym: 121/3.

[208] Mustadrak Hakim, vol.3, p.108; Al-Isābah fi Tamīz al-Sahābā, vol. 4, p.369.

that when the time of the death of Abu Tālib approached, Allāh's Messenger ﷺ went to him and found Abu Jahl bin Hishām and `Abdullah bin Abi Umayyah bin Al-Mughīra by his side. Allāh's Messenger ﷺ said to Abu Tālib:

يَا عَمِّ، قُلْ لاَ إِلَهَ إِلاَّ اللَّهُ، كَلِمَةً أَشْهَدُ لَكَ بِهَا عِنْدَ اللَّهِ

'O uncle, say "There is no god but Allāh", a sentence with which I shall be a witness [i.e. argue] for you before Allāh.'

Abu Jahl and `Abdullah bin Abi Umayyah said, "O Abu Tālib! Are you going to denounce the religion of `Abdul Muttalib?" Allāh's Messenger ﷺ kept on inviting Abu Tālib to say it [i.e. 'None has the right to be worshipped but Allāh'] while they [Abu Jahl and `Abdullah] kept on repeating their statement till Abu Tālib said as his last statement that he was on the religion of `Abdul Muttalib and refused to say, 'None has the right to be worshipped but Allāh.' Then Allāh's Messenger ﷺ said:

أَمَا وَاللَّهِ لأَسْتَغْفِرَنَّ لَكَ، مَا لَمْ أُنْهَ عَنْكَ

'I will keep on asking Allāh's forgiveness for you unless I am forbidden [by Allāh] to do so.' [209]

Another hadīth relates that Abu Tālib's words to the Holy Prophet ﷺ were:

لَوْلاَ أَنْ تُعَيِّرَنِي قُرَيْشٌ يَقُولُونَ إِنَّمَا حَمَلَهُ عَلَى ذَلِكَ الْجَزَعُ لأَقْرَرْتُ بِهَا عَيْنَكَ

Were it not the fear of the Quraysh blaming me [and] saying that it was the fear of [approaching death] that induced me to do so, I would have certainly delighted your eyes. [210]

---

[209] Bukhārī: 1360.
[210] Muslim: 25 b.

And so the Holy Prophet ﷺ grieved for his dear uncle and kept to his word and continued to ask for Abu Tālib's forgiveness until the following verses were revealed:

مَا كَانَ لِلنَّبِيِّ وَالَّذِينَ آمَنُوا أَن يَسْتَغْفِرُوا لِلْمُشْرِكِينَ وَلَوْ كَانُوا

أُولِي قُرْبَىٰ مِن بَعْدِ مَا تَبَيَّنَ لَهُمْ أَنَّهُمْ أَصْحَابُ الْجَحِيمِ ۞

It is not appropriate for the Prophet and the believers to seek forgiveness for the polytheists, even if they are kinsmen, after it became clear to them that they are the people of hell. [211]

And:

إِنَّكَ لَا تَهْدِي مَنْ أَحْبَبْتَ وَلَٰكِنَّ اللَّهَ

يَهْدِي مَن يَشَاءُ ۚ وَهُوَ أَعْلَمُ بِالْمُهْتَدِينَ ۞

You cannot give guidance to whomsoever you wish, but Allāh gives guidance to whomsoever He wills, and He best knows the ones who are the rightly guided. [212]

Allāh ﷻ alone knows who is worthy of receiving hidāyah and who is capable of maintaining faith. When the Messenger of Allāh ﷺ received this revelation, he stopped praying for them and was content with the will of Allāh ﷻ. It is reported that the noble companion, Bilāl bin Rabāh ﷺ, was overjoyed at the revelation of the verse above and was heard to glorify Allāh ﷻ, saying that it was because Allāh ﷻ had kept hidāyah in His hands that Bilāl ﷺ was able to reach such high station and advance so far ahead, otherwise the family of the Holy Prophet ﷺ would have been first in everything and Bilāl left behind.

Having said this, some years after the passing of Abu Tālib and after Hijrah, a mention was made of his uncle Abu Tālib before the Messenger of Allāh ﷺ and he said:

---

[211] Qur'ān 9:113.
[212] Qur'ān 28:56.

لَعَلَّهُ تَنْفَعُهُ شَفَاعَتِي يَوْمَ الْقِيَامَةِ فَيُجْعَلُ فِي
ضَحْضَاحٍ مِنْ نَارٍ يَبْلُغُ كَعْبَيْهِ يَغْلِي مِنْهُ دِمَاغُهُ

My intercession may benefit him on the Day of Resurrection and he may be placed in the shallow part of the Fire which would reach his ankles and his brain would be boiling. [213]

And, in another narration, he said:

أَهْوَنُ أَهْلِ النَّارِ عَذَابًا أَبُو طَالِبٍ وَهُوَ مُنْتَعِلٌ بِنَعْلَيْنِ يَغْلِي مِنْهُمَا دِمَاغُهُ

The Prophet ﷺ said: Among the inhabitants of the Fire Abu Tālib would have the least suffering, and he would be wearing two shoes [of Fire] which would boil his brain. [214]

So the company of the Holy Prophet ﷺ did benefit him, as he was saved from the worst of the punishment due to the Prophet ﷺ. Abu Tālib will, however, never be allowed to enter Jannah, as the key to Jannah is the declaration that there is no god but Allāh ﷻ.

Returning to our main topic, the word of hidāyah is assigned towards Allāh ﷻ as the prime giver of guidance in the verse, [اِهْدِنَا الصِّرَاطَ الْمُسْتَقِيمَ], however in other places the word hidāyah is linked to the Qur'ān itself:

إِنَّ هَٰذَا الْقُرْآنَ يَهْدِي لِلَّتِي هِيَ أَقْوَمُ وَيُبَشِّرُ الْمُؤْمِنِينَ الَّذِينَ يَعْمَلُونَ الصَّالِحَاتِ
أَنَّ لَهُمْ أَجْرًا كَبِيرًا ۞ وَأَنَّ الَّذِينَ لَا يُؤْمِنُونَ بِالْآخِرَةِ أَعْتَدْنَا لَهُمْ عَذَابًا أَلِيمًا ۞

Surely, this Qur'ān guides to something that is most straightforward, and gives glad tidings to the believers who do good deeds that ready for them there is a great reward,

---

[213] Bukhārī: 3885, 6564; Muslim: 210.

[214] Muslim 212.

and that We have prepared a painful punishment for those who do not believe in the Hereafter. [215]

Moreover, in another verse, hidāyah is assigned to and associated with the Holy Prophet ﷺ:

وَكَذَلِكَ أَوْحَيْنَا إِلَيْكَ رُوحًا مِّنْ أَمْرِنَا ۚ مَا كُنتَ تَدْرِي مَا الْكِتَابُ وَلَا الْإِيمَانُ وَلَٰكِن جَعَلْنَاهُ نُورًا نَّهْدِي بِهِ مَن نَّشَاءُ مِنْ عِبَادِنَا ۚ وَإِنَّكَ لَتَهْدِي إِلَىٰ صِرَاطٍ مُّسْتَقِيمٍ ۞ صِرَاطِ اللَّهِ الَّذِي لَهُ مَا فِي السَّمَاوَاتِ وَمَا فِي الْأَرْضِ ۗ أَلَا إِلَى اللَّهِ تَصِيرُ الْأُمُورُ ۞

In similar way, We have revealed to you a Spirit from Our command. You did not know earlier what was the Book or what was Īmān [true faith], but We have made it [the Qur'ān] a light with which We guide whomsoever We will from among Our servants. And indeed you are guiding [people] to a straight path, the path of Allāh, the One to whom belongs all that is in the heavens and all that is in the earth. Be aware that towards Allāh all matters shall finally return. [216]

GUIDANCE VARIES

Here it is important to differentiate between the roles of Allāh ﷻ, His Prophet ﷺ, and the Qur'ān in guiding and understand the different association each has with hidāyah. Hidāyah can carry two meanings: firstly, to show the path; and secondly to guide along the path. To guide someone and carry them along the path is in Allāh's control alone. However, showing the correct path is the role played by the Noble Qur'ān and the Beloved Prophet ﷺ, as well as Allāh ﷻ.

---

[215] Qur'ān 17:9-10.
[216] Qur'ān 42:52-53.

The Beloved Prophet ﷺ once said to a non-believer that he should say the Kalimah [The Declaration of Faith] and become a Muslim. The man asked why he should heed the Holy Prophet's ﷺ advice. The Holy Prophet ﷺ replied by asking the man to consider a situation such that the man was travelling, lost, stuck in the jungle, separated from his caravan and had no idea where he was. All around him, he could hear the frightening sounds of the wild, the fear-provoking screeches and howls of unseen animals and the unmistakable roars and growls of jungle cats. He had no sense of the direction he should take and felt penned in by dangers from every side, not knowing where it may lurk. He was mired in this fear and worry, when all of a sudden a man stepped out into the clearing. The man was of his same locality, and he knew him and trusted him. This second man beckoned him and guided him, telling him that he knew which path to take and he can guide him to safety. Would he go with this man or not?

The man replied to the Beloved Prophet ﷺ that of course he would go. The Beloved Prophet ﷺ said to him that this was his exact state right now. He was mired and trapped in the jungle of *Kufr* [Disbelief], which would lead to the chastisement of Jahannam. This would be worse than being devoured by wild beasts of the jungle. And the Beloved Prophet ﷺ said that he was like that man of his locality who had come to guide him, telling him to come with him so he could be saved and protected. Upon hearing this parable, the non-believer declared the sahadah. He was often heard thereafter saying that the Beloved Prophet ﷺ had placed such an argument before him that no room had remained for doubt or reply.

This is indeed the example of the Beloved Prophet ﷺ and the rest of mankind. He ﷺ guides us and shows us the path we need to take to escape the fears and horrors of *Kufr* that surround us, and when such a person comes to guide us we should accept his guidance.

SIRĀTE MUSTAQEEM

After this, we come to [الصِّرَاطَ الْمُسْتَقِيمَ] 'the straight path'. Allāh ﷻ Himself explains what is meant by 'the straight path' in the above mentioned verse, stating:

صِرَاطِ اللَّهِ الَّذِي لَهُ مَا فِي السَّمَاوَاتِ

وَمَا فِي الْأَرْضِ ۗ أَلَا إِلَى اللَّهِ تَصِيرُ الْأُمُورُ ۞

The path of Allāh, the One to whom belongs all that is in the heavens and all that is in the earth. Behold! To Allāh do all matters shall finally return. [217]

In other words, it is the path that leads to Allāh ﷻ and His mercy and pleasure without any deviation or distraction. It is a straight path, a path of *Taqwā* [constant awareness of Allāh ﷻ], in which all of His divine commandments are fulfilled and never shirked, and all forbidden things are left and distanced. It may be a difficult path to walk, having to act upon all the farāidh, Sunnah, and nawāfil; and having to stay away from every harām, makrūh, and mashkūk thing. Many of us struggle to maintain our Sunnah actions or even fall into the habits of makrūh and mashkūk actions. And as Mufti Sa'īd Pālanpūrī states, if we markdown our makrūh and mashkūk actions as minor, we will end up with a great mountain of makrūh actions for which we will be held to account.

One Hadīth narrated by Imām Tirmīdhī, Imām Nasai and Imām Ahmed, states the meaning of '*sirāt*':

Nawwās ibn Sam'aan ﷺ narrates that Rasūlullāh ﷺ set the parable of sirāte mustaqeem with a straight path. On both sides of the path are two walls in which doors are open, and on the doors are curtains hanging down. On the gateway to the path, is an announcer calling out, 'O people! Enter this highway, all together. And do not go crooked.' There is another caller at the top of the

---

[217] Qur'ān 42:53.

highway. When a person intends to open any of the doors along the highway, he calls out, 'Don't open it, because if you open it, you will end up going in.'

The highway is Islam. The walls on the sides are the limits set by Allāh ﷻ. The doors which are open, are gateways to the prohibitions [i.e matters which Allāh ﷻ has made harām]. The caller at the opening of the highway is the Book of Allāh ﷻ [Qur'ān]. The caller above [and along with those walking] is the admonisher provided by Allāh ﷻ in the heart of every Muslim.' [218]

Once, one Shaykh From India sat with me in the car. As the car moved, the seat belt warning starting to beep. Upon his enquiry, I said, 'This is like the admonisher in the heart. It keeps beeping slowly, then the beeping gets louder, then if a person doesn't obey, it completely goes silent.'

We also get a notification in our heart, every time we intend to do something wrong. If we take heed, it keeps reminding, otherwise it dies down after some time. When that happens, the person loses any guilty conscience which he might have had before. May Allāh ﷻ keep us steadfast in sirāte mustaqeem.

THE GREATEST MIRACLE IS BEING STEADFAST

It is said that a man served in the company of a pious shaykh for twenty years, after which one day he asked, 'Master, I have served you for two decades and have been your constant companion all these years. Yet, I have never seen you perform any miracles or be graced with any divine miraculous favours. And it is said of so-and-so pious shaykhs that they perform such feats as flying in the air. Why is this so?'

The shaykh replied, 'You have been with me these twenty years and have been my constant companion. In these twenty years, have you ever witnessed any occasion on which I have missed a Sunnah or even nafil action? Have you ever seen me even once perform a makrūh action? Have I ever done anything in these twenty years which went against the Sunnah?'

---

[218] Ibn Kathīr 1-24.

The man thought deeply and replied, 'No, Hadhrat. Never have you ever gone against the Sunnah. Indeed your whole life before me has been an example of the Sunnah.'

'Know then, this is Allāh's divine favour upon me and this is the greatest miracle.'

THE HADĪTH OF ISTIQAMAT

This is the true meaning of the 'straight path'. A life in complete accordance to Allāh's commandments and the teachings of our Beloved Prophet ﷺ. It is for this reason that it is narrated on the authority of Sufyān bin 'Abdullah al-Thaqafī ؓ that he said:

يَا رَسُولَ اللَّهِ حَدِّثْنِي بِأَمْرٍ أَعْتَصِمُ بِهِ . قَالَ قُلْ رَبِّيَ اللَّهُ ثُمَّ اسْتَقِمْ

I asked: "O Messenger of Allāh! Inform me about a matter that I may hold fast to." He [The Prophet ﷺ] said: 'Say: My Rabb is Allāh, then be steadfast.' [219]

Upon this, the mashāikh comment that:

الاستقامة خير من الف كرامة ،

و ما أكرم الله تعالي عبدا بكرامة خير من الاستقامة

Steadfastness is better than a thousand miraculous feats, and Allāh Ta'ālā has never blessed a servant with a miraculous favour better than steadfastness. [220]

Īmām Ghazālī ؒ is reported to have said: 'It is far easier to cross the Bridge of Sirāt, which is as thin as a hair and as sharp as a sword, than it is to remain steadfast upon the straight path in this world.'

---

[219] Tirmīdhī 2410; Ibn Mājah 3972; Muslim 38.
[220] *Al-Jawāhir al-Lu'luīyah Fī Sharhi al-Arba'īn an-Nawawīyah*: pg.183.

May Allāh 🕮 grant us all steadfastness and help us with this difficult task. May Allāh 🕮 protect us from falling into disobedience.

CONTROLLING ONE'S TONGUE

The biggest pitfall that we as Muslims fall into is the failure or inability to control our tongues. We need to refrain from all the sins of the tongue. We need to refrain especially from Ghībah [backbiting], which is a grave sin that we are all culpable of committing. Ghībah is to say something which would hurt a person's feelings, or which he/she would dislike to hear, in their absence and behind their back.

Some people say such things directly to the person and then say, 'Oh, we say it right on their face. We don't go behind their backs.' As if this absolves them and is okay. This is called Tuh'mah [false accusation] and worse than backbiting, and can be even more hurtful. Khalid bin Ma'dān 🕮 narrates from Mu'ādh bin Jabal 🕮 that the Messenger of Allāh 🕮 said:

$$\text{مَنْ عَيَّرَ أَخَاهُ بِذَنْبٍ لَمْ يَمُتْ حَتَّى يَعْمَلَهُ}$$

"Whoever shames his brother for a sin, he shall not die until he [himself] commits it."
[One of the narrators] Ahmad [bin Manī' 🕮] said: They said: 'From a sin he has repented from." [221]

I recall the incident of a young Imām who was employed and became popular with the people. The senior Imām became jealous of him and sought to drive a wedge between the young Imām and the congregation. He targeted the young Imām's wife, as she did not practice the full face veil, and began to say to the people, 'What kind of an Imām have you employed? Do you not see his wife

---

[221] Tirmīdhī: 2693; Bulūgh al-Marām: 1515.

who roams around the streets uncovered? How can you appoint a dayyuth [222] as your Imām?'

It so happened that the young Imām's wife eventually began to wear the niqāb and this senior Imām, who had sought to defame the young Imām, found his own wife discarding the niqāb.

We pray that Allāh ﷻ saves us from slandering and from backbiting, and from all the sins of the tongue. Imām Ghazālī ؒ has enumerated all the sins of the tongue in his masterwork, *Ihyā 'Ulūm al-Dīn*, which should be carefully studied.

WHY WE SHOULD KEEP ASKING FOR HIDĀYAT

Returning to the verse, 'Show us the straight path' [إِهْدِنَا الصِّرَاطَ الْمُسْتَقِيمَ], a question may arise here as to why must we ask for guidance when we already have guidance, we have Imān? Surely, those who have yet to say the Kalimah and make the declaration of faith should be the ones asking for guidance? The answer is that it is about remaining upon the straight path and being constantly guided along it, rather than merely being shown the path at the beginning. We often fall short or are distracted from the path, which is why Allāh ﷻ makes us ask for guidance five times a day throughout our lives. And if we keep to this, one day we might utter the words with true earnest and sincerity and Allāh ﷻ will open the doors of complete guidance for us.

We should ask for hidāyah and for Allāh ﷻ to make us follow the straight path, regardless of whether our *nafs* wants to or not. We should ask Allāh ﷻ to make us pray five times a day, in the masjid, to recite Qur'ān daily, to wear the hijāb and the niqāb, to stay away from time wasting pursuits, to stay away from spending hours in front of a television, regardless of whether our *nafs* likes it or not. The television should be avoided. And if you can't bring yourself to avoid it completely, then at least reduce the amount of viewing. Try to stay away from watching movies, and especially blue movies.

---

[222] Dayyuth is someone who approves illicit behaviour in his family.

PORNOGRAPHY

Pornography is one of the most despicable and disgusting inventions of the modern age. The one who falls into its addiction damages and scars his soul. It is the root cause of many personal and domestic problems, shattering lives and families. There are a great many cases where divorces have occurred because husbands have fallen prey to this perverse addiction. Allāh 🕮 protect us!

DUĀ FOR GUIDANCE

We should constantly pray for guidance:

اللهم اهدنا واهد بنا ²²³ واهد الناس جميعا

اللَّهُمَّ إن قلوبنا ونواصينا وجوارحنا بيدك لم تملكنا منها شيئا , فإذا فعلت ذلك بنا

فكن أنت ولينا واهدنا إلى سواء السبيل ²²⁴

Oh, Allāh! Guide us and make us a means of guidance, and guide all the people. Oh Allāh! Our hearts and minds and limbs are in Your control, and we have no authority over them. And as You have made it so, You are our protector, so guide us toward the straight path.

A SHORT COMPREHENSIVE DUĀ

Abu Mālik al-Ashja'ī 🕮 reports on the authority of his father that whenever a person embraced Islam, Allāh's Messenger 🕮 would teach him/her how to observe prayer and then command him/her to supplicate in these words:

---

223 Jāmi' Ma'mar bin Rāshid: 242.
224 Tārīkh Baghdād: 4464; Kanzul Ummāl: 3807, 3644.

اَللَّهُمَّ اغْفِرْ لِي وَارْحَمْنِي وَاهْدِنِي وَعَافِنِي وَارْزُقْنِي

'*O Allāh, forgive me, have mercy upon me, guide me, grant me safety and security,
and provide sustenance for me.*' *And then he would hold up four fingers and say,
'These combine your religious and worldly affairs.*' [225]

After asking Allāh ﷻ to be guided and shown the straight path, the next verse
elaborates on the straight path.

VERSE 6

صِرَاطَ الَّذِينَ أَنْعَمْتَ عَلَيْهِمْ ﴿٦﴾

The path of those on whom You have bestowed Your Grace.

THOSE FAVOURED BY ALLĀH ﷻ

As for the people upon whom Allāh ﷻ has bestowed His divine favour, they are
of four categories as mentioned in the verse of Sūrah Nisaa:

وَمَن يُطِعِ اللَّهَ وَالرَّسُولَ فَأُولَٰئِكَ مَعَ الَّذِينَ أَنْعَمَ اللَّهُ عَلَيْهِم مِّنَ النَّبِيِّينَ وَالصِّدِّيقِينَ
وَالشُّهَدَاءِ وَالصَّالِحِينَ ۚ وَحَسُنَ أُولَٰئِكَ رَفِيقًا ۝ ذَٰلِكَ الْفَضْلُ مِنَ اللَّهِ ۚ وَكَفَىٰ بِاللَّهِ

عَلِيمًا ۝

*Those who obey Allāh and the Messenger will be with those whom Allāh has blessed,
namely, the prophets, the Siddīqīn, the Shuhadā' and the righteous. And excellent are
they as companions. That grace is from Allāh; and Allāh is sufficient as being the One
who knows.* [226]

---

[225] Muslim: 2697 a, 2697 b, Muslim 2697 c; Ibn Mājah: 3845.
[226] Qur'ān 4:69-70.

As for 'the prophets' ﷺ, it is clear who they are and what is meant by them, and the doors of prophet-hood have been sealed after the final prophet, Muhammad ﷺ. The remaining three categories, 'the Siddīqīn, the Shuhadā', and the Sālihīn' have continued and are still continuing to prevail within the Ummah, and will continue to do so till the Day of Judgement.

SIDDĪQUES STILL REMAIN

Indeed, the doors to *Siddīqiyat* did not close after the death of our master, Sayyiduna Abu Bakr as-Siddīq ﷺ. In fact, Sayyiduna 'Ali ﷺ was heard to say during his khilāfah that:

أَنَا عَبْدُ اللَّهِ، وَأَخُو رَسُولِهِ صلى الله عليه وسلم وَأَنَا الصِّدِّيقُ الأَكْبَرُ،

لاَ يَقُولُهَا بَعْدِي إِلاَّ كَذَّابٌ صَلَّيْتُ قَبْلَ النَّاسِ بِسَبْعِ سِنِينَ

I am the slave of Allāh and the brother of His Messenger. I am the greatest teller of the truth [Siddīq Akbar], and no one will say this after me except a liar. I prayed seven years before the people. [227]

HADHRAT MARYAM ﷺ WAS A SIDDĪQAH

The noble lady, Maryam [Mary] ﷺ the mother of 'Īsā [Jesus] ﷺ is described as a Siddīqah in the following verse:

مَّا الْمَسِيحُ ابْنُ مَرْيَمَ إِلَّا رَسُولٌ قَدْ خَلَتْ مِن قَبْلِهِ

الرُّسُلُ وَأُمُّهُ صِدِّيقَةٌ ۖ كَانَا يَأْكُلَانِ الطَّعَامَ ۗ انظُرْ كَيْفَ

نُبَيِّنُ لَهُمُ الْآيَاتِ ثُمَّ انظُرْ أَنَّىٰ يُؤْفَكُونَ ۞

---

[227] Ibn Mājah: 125.

The Masīh, son of Maryam, is no more than a Messenger. There have been messengers before him. His mother was very truthful [a Siddīqah]. Both of them used to eat food. Look how We explain signs to them, then see how far they are turned away. [228]

HADHRAT Ā'ISHAH ﷞ WAS A SIDDĪQAH

From this we learn that the rank of a Siddīq is not gender exclusive and can be attained by both men and women. Another example of a woman who achieved the high rank of Siddīqiyat is the Mother of the Believers, the noble lady Ā'ishah ﷞:

وكان مسروق إذا روى عن عائشة قال : حدثتني الصديقة بنت الصديق حبيبةُ

رسول الله صلى الله عليه وسلم المبرأة من السماء أو قال حبيبة حبيب الله ، المبرأة

من فوق سبع سموات

Whenever Masrūq would narrate from our mother Ā'ishah ﷞, he would say, 'As-Siddīqah [Ā'ishah] bint as-Siddīq [Abu Bakr], the beloved of the beloved of Allāh [i.e. The Prophet ﷺ], the one whose innocence was declared from above the seven heavens, narrated this to me.' [229]

It is evident then that the doors to Siddīqiyat are still open, and the Siddīqīn exist and occur in every generation, and there are Siddīqīn amongst the Ummah even now.

Similar is the case with the martyrs and the righteous ones. They still remain and will continue to do so until the day of judgement. They are the ones favoured by Allāh ﷻ. We beg Allāh ﷻ to keep us on their path.

---

[228] Qur'ān 5:75.

[229] Mu'ālim at-Tanzīl (Concise Tafsīr Baghawī): p.648; Mukhtasar al-Ulūw' (Dhahabī): p. 128.

WHY 'THE PATH OF THOSE WHOM YOU FAVOURED?'

Another aspect of this verse to make note of is that it states, 'The path of those upon whom You have bestowed Your Grace', rather than 'the path of Qur'ān', or 'the path of Hadīth'. This points to the fact that there are people in every generation upon whom Allāh ﷻ bestows His Grace. They are knowledgeable, god-fearing and of sound character, whose company should be cherished and whose path should be followed. Every era and every area has such pious personalities and scholars who should be followed, they are the ones whom Allāh ﷻ has graced with His favour.

This rejects the claim of some people who say just to follow Sahīh Hadīth. They actually say, 'follow me'. i.e My interpretation of Hadīth. We should be very careful not to fall for such fancy slogans. Allāh ﷻ says:

$$وَاتَّبِعْ سَبِيلَ مَنْ أَنَابَ إِلَيَّ ۝$$

"Follow the path of those who turn towards Me." [230]

And:

$$آمِنُوا كَمَا آمَنَ النَّاسُ ۝$$

"Believe like the people have believed." [231]

We find in the Hadīth: 'Hold firmly to my Sunnah and the Sunnah of the rightly guided Khulafā. Bite on to it with your molar teeth.' [232] And also: 'Follow these two after me, Abubakr and Umar.' [233]

The Qur'ān says: 'Ask the people of the reminder if you do not know.'

---

[230] Qur'ān 31:15.
[231] Qur'ān 2:13.
[232] Ibn Mājah.
[233] Mishkāt, Ibn Mājah.

The Hadīth says:

يد الله على الجماعة ومن شذ شذ فى النار

'The hand of Allāh [i.e. His succor] is with the mass. And whosoever isolates,
isolates himself in the fire.' [234]

Qādhī Baidhāwī ﷺ writes: 'Even though the blessings of Allāh ﷻ are countless,
they can be summarised in two categories:

1. Dunyawī (related to this world).

2. Ukhrawī (related to the hereafter).

The first category is of two types:

1. Wahbī (gifted by Allah).

2. Kasbī (hard earned by man).

Wahbī is of two types:

1. Rūhānī (spiritual).

2. Jismānī (related to the body).

'Rūhani is like breathing a soul into the body, enlightening it with intellect and
whatever follows it, e.g. high levels of understanding, contemplating,
speaking.

'Jismānī is like creating the body, the strengths which are needed by the
body, and the conditions of the body, e.g. good health, complete limbs and
internal organs, such as the heart, liver, kidney, etc.

'Kasbī is cleansing the ego from its bad traits and beautifying it with good
traits, beautiful character and exemplary manners; also, beautifying the outer
body with appropriate clothing, and desirable beauty, acquiring good position
within society, earning a good livelihood and having enough wealth.

---

[234] Mishkāt.

'The second is that Allāh ﷻ forgives the shortcomings, and is pleased, and grants one an abode in the loftiest levels of Jannah among the angels that are blessed with proximity and with eternal life.

'In the above āyah, the second meaning seems to be the intended one, that Allāh ﷻ guides us along the path of those who have been favoured with this eternal bliss, and also those blessings from the first category, which are a means to reach this second one. This is because whatever is besides these things is gifted to a believer and non-believer alike.'

VERSE 7

غَيْرِ الْمَغْضُوبِ عَلَيْهِمْ وَلَا الضَّالِّينَ ﴿٧﴾

Not of those who have incurred Your wrath, nor of those who have gone astray.

The ones who incurred Allāh's ﷻ wrath and those who went astray were people from the previous nations of Yahood and Nasaara.

Adiyy Ibn Hātim ﷺ [who used to be a Christian before he embraced Islam] reports: 'I asked Rasūlullāh ﷺ regarding those with whom Allāh was angry. He replied, 'The Yahood, and the misguided ones were the Nasaara.'

There is an indication towards this in the Qur'ān. Allāh ﷻ says:

وَضُرِبَتْ عَلَيْهِمُ الذِّلَّةُ وَالْمَسْكَنَةُ وَبَاءُوا بِغَضَبٍ مِّنَ اللَّهِ ۚ ذَٰلِكَ بِأَنَّهُمْ كَانُوا يَكْفُرُونَ بِآيَاتِ اللَّهِ وَيَقْتُلُونَ النَّبِيِّينَ بِغَيْرِ الْحَقِّ ۚ ذَٰلِكَ بِمَا عَصَوا وَّكَانُوا يَعْتَدُونَ ۞

Then they [Israelites] were stamped with disgrace and misery, and they returned with wrath from Allāh. That was because they used to deny the signs of Allāh, and they would murder the prophets unjustly. That was because they disobeyed and transgressed all limits. [235]

---

[235] Qur'ān 2:61.

And:

ضُرِبَتْ عَلَيْهِمُ الذِّلَّةُ أَيْنَ مَا ثُقِفُوا إِلَّا بِحَبْلٍ مِّنَ اللَّهِ وَحَبْلٍ مِّنَ النَّاسِ وَبَاءُوا بِغَضَبٍ

مِّنَ اللَّهِ وَضُرِبَتْ عَلَيْهِمُ الْمَسْكَنَةُ ۚ ذَٰلِكَ بِأَنَّهُمْ كَانُوا يَكْفُرُونَ بِآيَاتِ اللَّهِ وَيَقْتُلُونَ

الْأَنبِيَاءَ بِغَيْرِ حَقٍّ ۚ ذَٰلِكَ بِمَا عَصَوا وَّكَانُوا يَعْتَدُونَ ❁

Disgrace has been stamped over them wherever they are found, unless [saved] through a source from Allāh and through a source from some people, and they have returned with wrath from Allāh, and misery has been stamped over them. All this is because they used to deny the signs of Allāh, and they used to murder the prophets unjustly. All this is because they disobeyed and transgressed the limits. [236]

And:

قُلْ هَلْ أُنَبِّئُكُم بِشَرٍّ مِّن ذَٰلِكَ مَثُوبَةً عِندَ اللَّهِ ۚ مَن لَّعَنَهُ اللَّهُ وَغَضِبَ عَلَيْهِ وَجَعَلَ

مِنْهُمُ الْقِرَدَةَ وَالْخَنَازِيرَ وَعَبَدَ الطَّاغُوتَ ۚ أُولَٰئِكَ شَرٌّ مَّكَانًا وَأَضَلُّ عَن سَوَاءِ السَّبِيلِ ❁

Say, "Shall I tell you about the ones whose retribution with Allāh is worse than that [which you deem bad]? They are those whom Allāh has subjected to His curse and to His wrath; and He has turned some of them into apes and swine, those who worshipped Tāghūt [Satan, the Rebel]. Those are worse in their situation, and far more astray from the straight path." [237]

And:

قُلْ يَا أَهْلَ الْكِتَابِ لَا تَغْلُوا فِي دِينِكُمْ غَيْرَ الْحَقِّ وَلَا تَتَّبِعُوا أَهْوَاءَ

---

[236] Qur'ān 3:112.
[237] Qur'ān 5:60.

قَوْمٍ قَدْ ضَلُّوا مِن قَبْلُ وَأَضَلُّوا كَثِيرًا وَضَلُّوا عَن سَوَاءِ السَّبِيلِ ❂

Say, O people of the Book, do not exceed the limits in your religion unjustly, and do not follow the desires of a people who have already gone astray, misled many and lost the right path. [238]

These verses refer only to the evil people from previous generations of Jews and Christians. As we know, good and bad people prevail in every era, in every nation, and every community. These were the bad people from those communities who reached excesses of sin and disobedience. There were good people among those nations too, and there are good and bad people in every community, including the current generations. The Noble Qur'ān goes into great detail describing the qualities of some of the pious Christians:

وَلَتَجِدَنَّ أَقْرَبَهُم مَّوَدَّةً لِّلَّذِينَ آمَنُوا الَّذِينَ قَالُوا إِنَّا نَصَارَىٰ ۚ ذَٰلِكَ بِأَنَّ مِنْهُمْ قِسِّيسِينَ وَرُهْبَانًا وَأَنَّهُمْ لَا يَسْتَكْبِرُونَ ❂ وَإِذَا سَمِعُوا مَا أُنزِلَ إِلَى الرَّسُولِ تَرَىٰ أَعْيُنَهُمْ تَفِيضُ مِنَ الدَّمْعِ مِمَّا عَرَفُوا مِنَ الْحَقِّ ۚ

You will certainly find that the closest of them in friendship with the believers are those who say, "We are Christians." That is because among them there are priests and monks, and because they are not arrogant. When they hear what has been sent down to the Messenger, you will see their eyes flowing with tears because of the truth they have recognized. [239]

And:

ثُمَّ قَفَّيْنَا عَلَىٰ آثَارِهِم بِرُسُلِنَا وَقَفَّيْنَا بِعِيسَى ابْنِ مَرْيَمَ وَآتَيْنَاهُ الْإِنجِيلَ

---

[238] Qur'ān 5:77.
[239] Qur'ān 5:82-83.

وَجَعَلْنَا فِي قُلُوبِ الَّذِينَ اتَّبَعُوهُ رَأْفَةً وَرَحْمَةً وَرَهْبَانِيَّةً ابْتَدَعُوهَا مَا كَتَبْنَاهَا عَلَيْهِمْ إِلَّا ابْتِغَاءَ رِضْوَانِ اللَّهِ فَمَا رَعَوْهَا حَقَّ رِعَايَتِهَا ۖ فَآتَيْنَا الَّذِينَ آمَنُوا مِنْهُمْ أَجْرَهُمْ ۖ وَكَثِيرٌ مِّنْهُمْ فَاسِقُونَ ۞

Then We made Our messengers follow them [Nuh and Ibrāhīm ﷺ] one after the other, then We sent after them 'Īsā, the son of Maryam [Jesus, son of Mary], and gave him the Injīl, and placed compassion and mercy in the hearts of those who followed him. As for monasticism, it was invented by them; We did not ordain it for them, but [they adopted it] to seek Allāh's pleasure, then could not observe it as was due. So We gave the believers from among them their reward. And many of them are sinners. [240]

Allāh ﷻ also says:

وَلَوْ أَنَّ أَهْلَ الْكِتَابِ آمَنُوا وَاتَّقَوْا لَكَفَّرْنَا عَنْهُمْ سَيِّئَاتِهِمْ وَلَأَدْخَلْنَاهُمْ جَنَّاتِ النَّعِيمِ ۞ وَلَوْ أَنَّهُمْ أَقَامُوا التَّوْرَاةَ وَالْإِنجِيلَ وَمَا أُنزِلَ إِلَيْهِم مِّن رَّبِّهِمْ لَأَكَلُوا مِن فَوْقِهِمْ وَمِن تَحْتِ أَرْجُلِهِم ۚ مِّنْهُمْ أُمَّةٌ مُّقْتَصِدَةٌ ۖ وَكَثِيرٌ مِّنْهُمْ سَاءَ مَا يَعْمَلُونَ ۞

And if the People of the Book were to believe and were conscious of Allāh, We would remove from them their misdeeds, and admit them into gardens of bliss. And if they would uphold the Torah, the Bible, and what has been revealed to them from their Rabb [this Qur'ān], they would eat from above them and from beneath their feet. Among them are the moderate [on the straight path], while many of them are carrying out evil acts. [241]

---

[240] Qur'ān 57:27.
[241] Qur'ān 5:65-66.

QĀDHĪ BAIDHĀWĪ'S BEAUTIFUL EXPLANATION

Qādhī Baidhāwī ﷺ explains that deviation from the straight path can either be deliberate or by mistake, yet the variations between them is great. As for those of the Jewish people who earned Allāh's ﷻ wrath and anger, it was because they had the Torah as well as living prophets amongst them. Despite these two clear sources of guidance, they deliberately went against the injunctions of Allāh ﷻ and knowingly caused mischief and evil on the earth.

As for the Christians who went astray, it was due to ignorance and misplaced zeal rather than any wicked or spiteful intent. Those who incurred wrath did so because they recognised the truth but went against it. And those who went astray did so because they tried to do good in accordance with their own desires rather than the guidance which was given to them. This caused them to transgress beyond limits. [242]

Even amongst the Muslim Ummah there are those who fall into these two categories, despite declaring the sahadah. Some who transgress deliberately, incurring Allāh's ﷻ anger; others who transgress through misplaced fervour and ignorance, leading themselves astray. For example, there are those who know Allāh's ﷻ injunctions and commands, yet still do not pray their salāh, or fast in Ramadhān, or who deliberately remain in a state of major impurity. Then, there are others who exceed limits in their fervour, invent innovations and fall into acts of ignorance close to idolatry. We pray that Allāh ﷻ saves us from both categories.

A COMPARISON BETWEEN SŪRAH FĀTIHA AND OTHER PRAYERS

In Tafsīr Haqqānī, the author delves into comparative religion and compares the prayer of Sūrah Fātiha to the 'Lord's Prayer' according to Christian

---

[242] Tafsīr Baidhāwī: pp. 11-12.

scriptures, comparing what is being sought and the manner of asking. The Lord's Prayer reads thus:

Our Father in heaven, hallowed be Your name. Your kingdom come.
Your will be done, on earth, as it is in heaven. Give us each day our daily bread.
And forgive us our sins, as we also have forgiven our debtors.
And lead us not into temptation, but deliver us from the evil one. [243] [244]

Shaykh Haqqānī takes issue with the phrases 'Give us each day our daily bread' and 'forgive us our sins, as we also have forgiven our debtors'. Firstly, Shaykh Haqqānī posits that when one stands before Allāh ﷻ, he/she should ask for the great and most important things, such as guidance towards the straight and correct path to His mercy, rather than just our daily bread which Allāh ﷻ has already taken on Himself and He is providing it anyway. Secondly, to say 'as we also have forgiven our debtors' or 'for we ourselves forgive everyone who is indebted to us' is disrespectful, as we do not always forgive and can often be intolerant and exacting. Allāh ﷻ, however, is the Most Merciful and the Oft Forgiving, His levels of mercy, compassion, and forgiveness are beyond compare. To say 'forgive as we forgive' is to claim a degree of superiority in these qualities. This is extremely disrespectful, and points that this prayer is most likely not the actual words taught by Īsā ﷺ, as he would not employ such wordings, but the interpretation of others who corrupted his teachings. The words of Sūrah Fātiha are not the words of some shaykh or scholar, not even the words of the Beloved Prophet ﷺ, but the direct words of Allāh ﷻ. May

---

[243] Matthew 6: 9-13; Luke 11: 2-4.
[244] Some manuscripts (Matthew 6:13) add: *For Yours is the kingdom and the power and the glory, forever. Amen.*

Allāh ﷻ protect our deen and give us the ability to be respectful towards Allāh ﷻ.

SAYING ĀMĪN UPON THE COMPLETION OF SŪRAH FĀTIHA

Once we finish Sūrah Fātiha, we say 'Āmīn', which is a way of pleading with Allāh ﷻ and begging, 'O Allāh, please make it so.' Often times, the duā itself does not carry so much weight, because the person praying does so absent-mindedly and distractedly, but the Āmīns of the congregation raise the duā to a level of acceptance. Therefore, we should say Āmīn after this sūrah and to say Āmīn here is Sunnah, both within salāh and outside salāh. As to whether it should be said loudly or silently during salāh, there is some difference of opinion amongst scholars. Imām Shafi'ī and Imām Ahmad are of the opinion that to say Āmīn loudly is the more preferred Sunnah; Imām Mālik and Imām Abu Hanīfah are of the opinion that to say it silently is the more preferred Sunnah. The Beloved Prophet ﷺ said Āmīn in both manners. According to Imām Abu Hanīfah's research, the Beloved Prophet ﷺ said Āmīn loudly on some occasions as a form of teaching and would otherwis say it silently. This is often made into a hugely contentious issue, where the reality is there is leeway for either side. It is best to not be in the extreme on either side.

Finally, there are two ways in which Āmīn can be said: either Āmīn, stretching the first vowel; or Amīn without any stress on the first vowel. Unstretched is closer to the Hebrew/Aramaic pronunciation. Qādhī Baidhāwī gives a proof for the stretched first vowel through the tale of Majnūn and his Layla. Majnūn's father takes him on pilgrimage to Makkah, to seek Allāh's ﷻ help in freeing him from the despondent madness his love has driven him to, but Majnūn takes hold of the Ka'ba's cloth and cries:

يا رب لا تَسْلُبَنِي حُبَّها أبداً ، وَيَرْحَمُ اللَّه عَبْداً قال آمينا

O Rabb, do not ever bereave me of her love!
And shower mercy upon him who says Āmīn!

VARIOUS MASĀ'IL REGARDING SŪRAH FĀTIHA

Question

Do we have to say Āmīn whenever we hear Sūrah Fātiha or is it only limited to Salāh?

Answer

Āmīn should be uttered whenever one reads Sūrah Fātiha and also when one hears another person read it. Imām Bukhārī has narrated on the authority of Abu Hurairah that Rasūlullāh said: 'When a person says Āmīn, the angels also say Āmīn. If his Āmīn coincides with the Āmīn of the angels, his previous sins will be forgiven.' [245]

In the narration of Muslim, it is stated, 'When the reciter says Āmīn, then say Āmīn...'

Hāfiz bin Hajar says in Fathūl Bārī that the first Hadīth shows that Āmīn should be said when <u>reciting</u> Sūrah Fātiha whether in Salāh or not, and the second one shows that Āmīn should be said when <u>hearing</u> the Sūrah whether in Salāh or not.

The meaning of Āmīn is 'O Allāh accept!' Sūrah Fatiha consists of Duā, so whenever Sūrah Fātiha is recited or heard, Āmīn should be said. During duās, Āmīn should be said with conviction.

---

[245] Bukhārī 781.

It is narrated in a Hadīth in Sunan Abū Dāwūd: 'Jibra'īl ﷺ taught me to say Āmīn at the end of Sūrah Fātiha and he said that it is like the seal upon a letter.'

Question

Why is it, that in some Mosques, Āmīn isn't said loud enough? And in other Mosques, Āmīn is said loudly. I would very much appreciate if you could tell me if we should say Āmīn loudly or not?

Answer

It is desirable to say Āmīn whenever you hear Sūrah Fātiha because Sūrah Fātiha is a duā, and this will be the case with all duās. Whenever duā is made, join in and say 'Āmīn'. Whenever a group of people gather and one of them makes duā and others say 'Āmīn', Allāh ﷻ accepts their duā – this is in the Hadīth. According to Imām Abu Hanifa's ﷺ research and Imām Mālik's ﷺ research, it would be more desirable to say it silently. This was the practice of the majority of the Sahābā ﷺ. According to the research of Imām Shāfi'ee ﷺ and Imām Ahmad Ibn Hanbal ﷺ, it is better to say it with a soft voice. No one allows screaming in the masjid.

Question

In the Qur'ān, there is no written Āmīn after Sūrah Fātiha, then why are we saying 'Āmīn' in Salāh?

Answer

You are right. This is one of the reasons why Imām Abu Hanifā ﷺ says that we should say Āmīn silently, so that it does not become part of the Qur'ān.

Question

Our Īmām during Fardh salāh forgot to recite Sūrah Fātiha and instead recited Sūrah Ikhlaas, he then went into rukū, and after finishing rukū, he remembered that he forgot Sūrah Fātiha. He then abandoned salāh and asked everyone to start again. Could he have continued and performed Sajdāh-e-Sahw instead of repeating the salāh?

Answer

He should have continued salāh and performed Sajdāh-e-sahw as reading Sūrah Fātiha is wājib. Missing a wājib forgetfully can be compensated with Sajdāh-e-Sahw.

Question

Does Sūrah Fātiha need to be recited in every rak'āt of nawaafil salāh?

Answer

Yes. This is because in nawaafil salāh, every two rak'āts are regarded as separate units, so you have to read Qur'ān in every rak'āt.

Question

When we read Sūrah Fātiha whilst reciting the Qur'ān, do we have to say 'Āmīn' at the end of the Sūrah? After saying Āmīn, do we recite Ta'awwuz and/or Tasmīyyah when starting Sūrah Baqarah?

Answer

Saying Āmīn upon completing Sūrah Fātiha is a Sunnah. Āmīn means 'O Allāh, please accept our duā.' During the salāh, the Hanafīs and Mālikī's say that it is more desirable to say it silently, whereas the Shafiee's and Hanbalī's say that it is more preferable to say it with a bit of voice. When you are continuing recitation, the first Ta'awwuz is enough. Bismillāh is sufficient to carry on with Sūrah Baqarah.

Question

When is one supposed to say *bismillahirrahmanirahim* in prayers?

Answer

In Salāh, a person should recite bismillāh before Sūrah Fātiha, and according to some also before reciting any other Sūrah. If after Sūrah Fātiha, one recites from the middle of a Sūrah, then he doesn't have to say bismillāh.

GLOSSARY

A

Āfiyat: Security

Al Hayy: The Ever Living

Alhamdulillāh: All praises are due to Allāh ﷻ

Akhirah: The hereafter

Āmīn: O Allāh, accept our invocation

Ashraful makhlūqāt: The best of all of Allāh's ﷻ creation

Auliyā: A Saint or Holy Person

Āyah: Verse

B

Bismillāh: In the name of Allāh ﷻ

D

Dāmat Barakātuhum: May his blessing be eternal

Deen: Religion

Dhikr: Remembrance of Allāh ﷻ

Dirham: Unit of currency

Duā: Supplication/Prayer

Dunyā: World

F

Fardh/Farāidh: Compulsory

Fiqh: Jurisprudence (The understanding and application of Islamic ideas, laws, commandments, etc. from the original sources of Shari'ah)

H

Hadīth: (Plural: Ahadīth) originally means a piece of news, story, or a report relating to a past or present event. In Islamic scholarship, it stands for the report of the words and deeds, approval and disapproval of Rasūlullāh ﷺ, i.e. the speech, action, or consent of the Holy Prophet ﷺ.

Hājī: A Muslim who has completed the Holy Pilgrimage (Hajj)

Hajj: Pilgrimage to Makkāh, involving visits to Mina, Arafah, and Muzdalifa. It is compulsory to perform it at least once in a lifetime for those who are able to undertake the journey monetarily and physically.

Halāl: Lawful, Permissible

Hanafī: Sunni Muslims who follow the school of thought of Imām Abu Hanīfa ﷴ

Hanbalī: Sunni Muslims who follow the school of thought of Imām Ahmed Ibn Hanbal

Haqīqat: Truth

Harām: Unlawful, Not permissible

Hidāyah: Guidance

Hijrah: Migration

I

Iblīs: The name given to Shaytān (the Devil)

Iftār: The time when one's fast is broken

Ihsān: Literally, it means to do good, show favour, or be kind. Thereafter, it is used for worshipping Allāh ﷻ with complete humbleness and His constant remembrance. Hadīth-e-Jibrā'īl ﷺ defines it thus: 'That you worship Allāh as though you are looking at Him, and if you do not see Him, then He is surely watching you.'

Īmān: Faith, Belief

Inshā-Allāh: If Allāh wills

J

Jahannam: Hell

Jannah: Paradise

Jinn: A creation created by Allāh from fire

Juz: Chapter

K

Kāmilīn: Saints, people who have rectified their souls and their actions, and have gained closeness to Allāh 🌟

Ka'ba: The house of Allāh, a square edifice built by the Prophet Ibrāhīm ﷺ and his son, Prophet Ismā'īl ﷺ in Makkah

Khilāfah: Caliph

Kufr: Disbelief

M

Makkāh: The holiest city of Islam

Makrūh: Disliked

Malā'ikah: Angels

Mashkūk: Those things that are doubtful

Masjid: Mosque

Masnoon: Sunnah of the Holy Prophet ﷺ

Muhaddith: Narrator of Hadīth, representative of the science or study of Hadīth, one learned in Ahadīth

Mu'min: A believer

N

Nabī: Prophet

Nafl: (Plural: Nawāfil) Optional

Nafs: Inner self

Nūr: Light

P
Pāra(s): Chapter(s)

Q
Qadhā: Making up for missed prayers/fasts, etc.
Qalandar: A wandering ascetic Sufi; a title given to a saint who is at a very high level of spirituality; one freed from ties to society, who lives in solitude
Qiblah: The direction in which a Muslim turns in prayer, which is facing the Ka'ba in Makkāh.
Qiyāmah: The Day of Judgement
Qur'ān: The final word of God Almighty, compiled in its original form up to this date.
Qurb: Closeness

R
Rabb: Lord
Rahma: Mercy
Rajab: The 7th Islamic month
Rak'ah: Unit of prayer
Ramadhān: The 9th Islamic month, the month of observing fasting
Rasūl: Messenger
Rizq: Sustenance

S
Sadaqah: Charity
Safr: Journey
Sahābā: The noble companions of the Holy Prophet ﷺ
Sajdāh: Prostration
Salaf: Predecessors
Salāh: Prayer
Sālihīn: Those who are pious

Shafi'ī: Those who follow the school of thought of Imām Shafi'ī ﷺ
Shari'ah: Islamic code
Shaytān: The Devil
Shaykh: A learned man, a scholar, a mentor, teacher
Shifā: Cure
Shirk: Associating partners with Allāh
Shuhadā: Martyrs
Shukr: To be thankful
Siddīqīn: Those who are truthful
Subhān-Allāh: Glory be to Allāh, Allāh is without blemish
Sunnah: The way of the Prophet ﷺ
Sūrah: Chapter

T̤
Tafsīr: Exegesis, most often used to describe the commentary of the Holy Qur'ān
Taqwā: Piety, constant awareness of Allāh ﷻ
Tasbīh: Glorification of Allāh ﷻ
Tawakkul: Trust
Tawheed: To confirm the oneness of Allāh ﷻ
Tawfeeq: Ability
Tilaawat: Recitation

U
Ulamā: Religious Scholars
Ummah: Nation

W
Wudhū: Ablution

Z

Zakāt: Charity, 2.5% of surplus wealth, which a Muslim should give to the poor, once in the whole year.

Zinā: Adultery